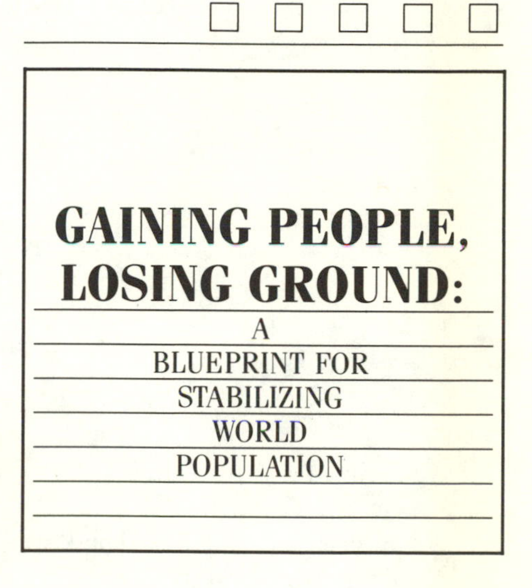

GAINING PEOPLE, LOSING GROUND:

A BLUEPRINT FOR STABILIZING WORLD POPULATION

THE POPULATION INSTITUTE
WASHINGTON, D.C.

SCIENCE PRESS
EPHRATA, PENNSYLVANIA

Second Printing *March 1990*

Design and Typography by Rings-Leighton, Ltd., Washington, D.C.
This book was composed in Fenice.

Printed in the United States of America by
Science Press, Ephrata, Pennsylvania.

Library of Congress Catalog Card Number: 87-62205
ISBN 0-9619165-1-6

The Population Institute
110 Maryland Avenue, N.E.
Washington, D.C. 20002
(202) 544-3300

CONTENTS

APPENDICES AND TABLES

ACKNOWLEDGMENTS

I would like to acknowledge my indebtedness to a number of academic professionals who reviewed drafts of this book and offered their criticisms and suggestions. I have had the pleasure of working with most of these faculty members during my travels on the college lecture circuit and they have been unfailingly gracious and accommodating.

Their comments on an earlier draft of this manuscript were most perceptive. While I am, of course, very appreciative of their assistance, it is the reader who will benefit most from their contributions.

The faculty reviewers represent a wide range of academic disciplines, including Sociology, Geography, Political Science, History, and Biology. They were: Donald W. Bogie of Auburn University at Montgomery; A.P. Garbin and Stewart Tolnay of the University of Georgia; Thomas Gustafson of California State University; Cindy Hull, Richard Santer, and Yvonne Vissing of Ferris State College; T.W. Jentsch of Kutztown University; William Kory of the University of Pittsburgh at Johnstown; Kooros Mahmoudi of Northern Arizona University; Myron M. Miller of St. Petersburg Junior College; Robert Oberst of Nebraska Wesleyan University; Eric A. Wagner of Ohio University; and Joseph S. Wood of the University of Nebraska at Omaha.

In addition, two people deserve special recognition. James Brackett, an internationally recognized demographer, made an invaluable contribution to this manuscript by offering data and expert advice. The information he provided has made this document a far more valuable resource.

I would also like to extend a special thanks to David Meyer, whose efforts through every stage of this project—from drafting to editing to final preparation of the manuscript—truly made this book possible.

Finally, it is worth emphasizing that the opinions reflected in this book's final form remain solely my own and any criticisms should be directed at me and not at any of those who generously agreed to offer their academic and editorial advice.

Werner Fornos

This book is dedicated to Reimert T. Ravenholt, M.D., an inspiring mentor and cherished friend who guided the U.S. Agency for International Development's Office of Population through its turbulent early years. His intellect, vision and courage, tempered by Midwestern farmboy horse sense, enable him to work on constructive solutions while others are still grappling to understand the problem.

INTRODUCTION

The population explosion is no longer a prediction. It is a reality. The world increased by 93 million people in 1989, enough people to create a new Pittsburgh, Pennsylvania—387,490—every day of the year. And although this actually represents a slowing of the population growth rate, consider that 40 percent of the developing world's population is under the age of 15. Three billion young people will enter their reproductive years in the next generation.

Overpopulation produces a terrible irony: having babies produces more suffering and, frequently, more death. This year alone we will witness the tragic deaths of 15 million infants—42,000 every day—all of whom will die before reaching their first birthday. Many of those children will die because their mothers did not know how to allow appropriate intervals between pregnancies, or did not have access to the family planning supplies to ensure proper spacing.

Moreover, 1,400 women die every day from the complications of pregnancy and abortion. Childbirth itself can be a life-threatening experience, all the more so in developing nations where proper health care can be hard to come by. Many of those 1,400 deaths would not occur if their victims did not face unwanted pregnancies.

By no later than the year 2020, the combined populations of Asia and Africa will be between six and eight billion, significantly more than now inhabit the entire planet. If the growth rate increases, we could be fighting for food, space, and shelter with 15 billion people within the next century.

The miseries and troubling consequences of rapid world population growth are clear. But we do not have to resign ourselves to this suffering. A concerted international effort to provide family planning information and the resources necessary to prevent unwanted pregnancies can improve the quality of life for millions now alive and billions yet to be born. The chief obstacle to building that effort is ignorance—ignorance on the part of Third World couples about the means and benefits of family planning and ignorance on the part of Americans and other Westerners about the threat of overpopulation.

This book has been written in an attempt to reduce that second ignorance. It is offered in the hope that it will present clearly and concisely the facts about global population growth and its implications, and with the confidence that Americans, presented with the evidence, will rise to the task of confronting the problem.

Morris K. Udall (D-Arizona)
Chairman, Committee on Interior and Insular Affairs
U.S. House of Representatives
Washington, D.C.
September 1987

GAINING PEOPLE, LOSING GROUND

1

WORLD BANK

Ugandan families at a famine relief camp

□□□□□

When the world's population soared past the five-billion mark recently, the public announcement merited a five-inch mention on the bottom of page B-8 of the New York Times. There were public expressions of concern, calls for action, and a brief flurry of newspaper editorials. But the attention soon faded and the world returned to what some say the world does best—reproducing itself.

In 1989 alone, the world added another 93 million people to its numbers. By the time this day is out, still another 394,800 human beings will have been born onto this planet. These numbers are at first startling; eventually, however, they can become numbing.

For more than 20 years the demographic trends of world population and its likely impact on the world's economy, environment, and human community have been clear. And yet public understanding of these issues remains limited.

Chief among the reasons why Americans tend to avoid confronting the issues related to world population growth is the intimidating scope of the problem. Like the number of dollars in the national debt, the issues of population are defined in billions and multiple millions, and their sheer size can blur comprehension and inspire avoidance.

And yet if we permit the six-billion mark or the eight-billion mark to pass casually as we have the fifth, our children will pay the price. For the world they inherit from us will be one in which the nations of the developing world will have lost the struggle for economic self-sufficiency. Staggering under the weight of huge and impoverished populations, having overtaxed and depleted their once-renewable natural resources, many of these nations would descend into a fierce cycle of economic deterioration and political and social instability.

Such conditions would have a direct and indisputable impact on the nations of the industrialized Northern Hemisphere as well. Americans, Canadians, Japanese, and Europeans would see their societies transformed by the pressures created by social and economic disintegration in the neighboring Third World, pressures that could well unhinge Western economies and undermine international security.

This bleak scenario does not arise from any defeatism or cynicism. Rather, it is founded on the most objective and realistic demographic data available and on science's best knowledge of the relationships between population and world environment. And it is offered in stark contrast to the striking opportunities and possibilities we now have for a far brighter international future. For the fate of the world is not sealed; it is being determined by the choices and decisions we are now making.

WORLD BANK

Third World urbanization means more traffic in Calcutta

The issue of world population growth is too often associated with pessimism. It is lumped together with environmental collapse and nuclear annihilation as just another way in which the earth may meet some horrible and violent end. This is unfortunate because a sense of gloom can deter us from doing something about it. We ensure our demise only by surrendering to it.

World population actually should be some cause for optimism, because it is one social issue that we can really do something about. It is true that the consequences of inaction would be grim, but it is just as true that the world today possesses all the tools it needs to bring population growth into a more stable pattern. In this sense, world population growth is not so much a problem as it is a challenge.

We are today at a critical juncture. The Free World still stands as a positive example of prosperity and opportunity to much of the developing world. And, just as important, the nations of the Third World can still reasonably expect to follow that example of economic development. Although their success in reaching economic self-sufficiency has been slower in coming than some imagined 20 or 30 years ago—hampered in part by booming population growth—the economies and often rich natural resources of many of these developing nations remain strong and plentiful enough to propel their populations toward greater prosperity.

That goal is clearly essential to a stable, democratic world. Achieving that end, however, will require sustained assistance from industrialized Western nations, wise economic planning, and, not least of all, responsible strategies for limiting population expansion.

This book presents a set of options. One option is inaction or inadequate action, and we will explore the consequences of that course. Another option is contained in the realistic short-term and long-term recommendations offered here. This book will also explore the more encouraging consequences of adopting these recommendations.

At bottom, this book lays out alternative costs—the costs on the one hand of meeting the unmet need for family planning services around the world and the costs on the other hand of ignoring that need. For industrialized countries such as the United States, the additional expenses required to help meet global family planning needs would be measured in tens of millions of dollars annually, a modest amount compared to hundreds of billions in potential damage to the world economy by unchecked population growth. But if the contrast between the alternative monetary costs of action and inaction is compelling, the difference in human costs—in lives saved, misery spared, hunger avoided, and fulfillment realized—is riveting. It will not cost a great deal of money to extend to the world's poor couples the means they need to decide for themselves the size of their families. And, if we are willing to make that investment now, we can secure for our children, and their children, a far happier and more hospitable world.

FAO

Third World hopes depend on curbing rapid population growth

□ □ □ □ □

CHART I: The World's Population Growth: Past and Projected

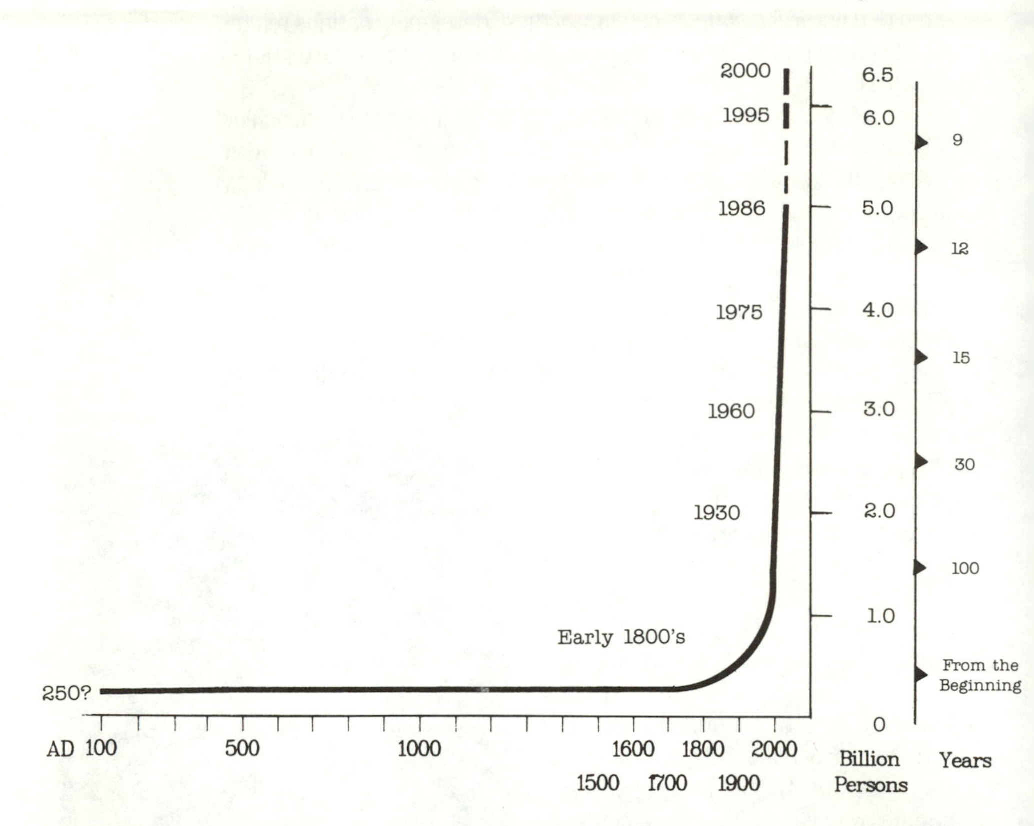

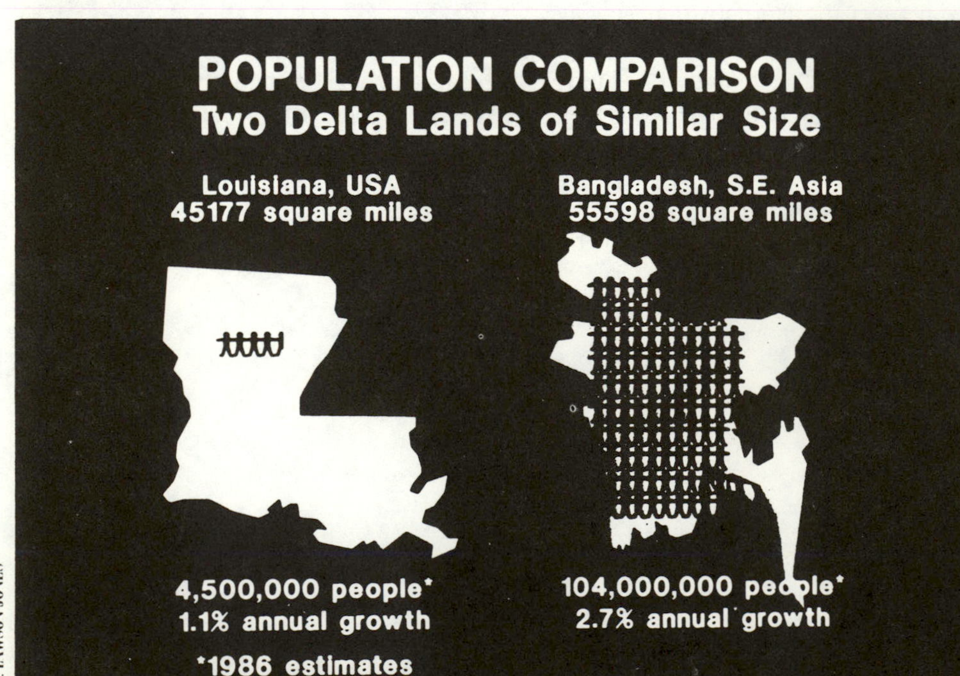

WHERE WE STAND NOW: RECENT POPULATION TRENDS

The "population crisis" is of very recent origin. Population is stable, of course, when birth and death rates are roughly equal, when the number of people who die each day matches the number of people born. The number of people inhabiting the earth remained quite stable from earliest recorded history through the Renaissance in the 1500s, a period of more than 4,000 years. Throughout that long period, the world's birth rate remained very high, but was necessarily so because the death rate was equally high. Despite occasional surges in births or deaths with the occurrence of good harvests or epidemics, the net result over time was very slow and steady population growth.

The picture began to change, however, in the 1800s, when industrialization and improvements in nutrition, agriculture, sanitation and medicine began to lower the death rate dramatically. Death rates fell first in the industrialized nations of Europe and North America, and because birth rates were slower to adjust, population then began to grow markedly. Simply stated, more people were surviving into adulthood and adults were living longer. Eventually, however, these nations reduced their birth rates in concert with rising standards of living, and population growth slowed so that today it is negligible across Europe and only slightly greater in North America.

This movement—starting with high but balanced birth and death rates, followed by imbalance as deaths decline, and completed when birth rates fall to restore balance at a lower level—is known as "the demographic transition." In the 1950s, academicians believed that Third World nations would follow the industrialized world in making this transition to economic development and stable population. These observers did not anticipate, however, that as many as 100 developing countries would become lodged in a "holding pattern" in the middle stage, with still-high birth rates and lowered death rates. This stage is characterized by rapid population growth, which strains the resources of pre-industrial economies and dilutes any modest gains realized in the national economic product. The longer these countries remain in this stage, and the more their populations swell as a result, the more difficult it becomes for them to achieve economic development and complete "the demographic transition" to industrialized economies and stable populations.

The doubling time for many of these developing countries—that is, the number of years required for a given population to double its size—is less than a single generation. The populations of Kenya, Jordan, Iran, Honduras, Haiti, and Vietnam, as only a few examples, will require no more than 20 years to double their populations at present growth rates. The total population of the entire African continent will double in just 24 years if current growth continues.

Those statistics are in stark contrast to demographic trends in the industrialized Northern Hemisphere. Population growth in Europe leveled off after World War II. In recent years, a handful of European nations, namely West Germany, Denmark, and Hungary, have actually experienced small reductions in their populations. And virtually every other European nation has achieved or approaches zero population growth. Although the United States and Canada have been somewhat slower to scale back their growth rates, and although the United States is presently experiencing something of a "baby boomlet," North America's population growth rate too has slowed to a modest 0.7 percent. At present growth rates, it would take the United States more than 100 years to double its population, and Italy's stable population will not double itself for another thousand years.

UNITED NATIONS

In the Third World, people are living longer: A Tibetan woman and her great-grandchild

7

DECLINE AND DESTABILIZATION: CHARACTERISTICS OF PRESENT GROWTH

The result of this discrepancy between booming Third World population growth and rather stable industrialized populations can be seen in a current worldwide demographic snapshot. The world's population of 5 billion will double itself in 40 years if current growth rates continue. A full 91 percent of that growth will occur in the developing world—in precisely the nations that can least afford to support that kind of expansion.

And as the size of world population increases, the time required to add the next billion people decreases. For world population to grow from 1 billion to 2 billion people, for example, took a century (1830 to 1930). Growth from 2 billion to 3 billion took 30 years (1930 to 1960), despite the fact that the world fought the most destructive war in human history during this interval. The fourth billion arrived in only 15 years (1975). The fifth in 11 years (1986). And the sixth billion may take as little as nine years (1995). This soaring growth is illustrated in Chart 1 on Page 4.

This accelerating growth is the inevitable result of "population momentum." Once a pattern of rapid growth is established, causing the number of young people to balloon, then even if fertility is radically curbed, it will still require several generations for that "bulge"—all of whom are potential parents themselves to yet more children—to work its way through the population cycle. Consequently, even if recent gains can be extended throughout the Third World, an ambitious and uncertain goal, world population would continue to grow and would not peak until at least the year 2050. And then the stabilized population could be anywhere from a low of 7.4 billion to an incredible 12.4 billion, depending on how successful we are in the immediate future in changing present growth patterns.

Pressures on Cities

A great deal of that population growth will take place in the Third World's congested urban centers. The population of the Third World as a whole is increasing by a significant 2.1 percent each year, but the population of the Third World's cities is growing by a swift 3.5 percent annually—fully three times as fast as the industrialized world's urban centers. Africa's cities are growing fastest, at a runaway 5 percent each year. The slum squatter settlements associated with these centers are growing at twice the rate of the cities themselves.

Many Third World cities are already clogged by people who migrated from depressed rural areas in search of job opportunities. Unskilled and finding few jobs once they arrived, these rural migrants often have ended up settling in squalid shantytowns surrounding the cities. As these urban centers have swelled with the unemployed and the homeless, their populations have stretched fragile local economies in which food, shelter, drinking water, and fuel are already in short supply.

Urban congestion and unemployment have pushed a number of developing nations to launch relocation programs (some of which are more voluntary than others) designed to encourage the resettlement of urban dwellers to sparsely populated and undeveloped rural areas. Indonesia, Egypt, Tanzania, Ethiopia, and Brazil, among others, have initiated resettlement programs. Each such program, however, has met with only limited success, in some cases because of resistance in the target population and in some cases because the lands chosen for settlement were unproductive or nonarable areas simply unable to support sizeable local populations.

UNITED NATIONS

Shacks in the shadow of affluence in Bombay

And yet the problems of urban congestion, already formidable in the Third World, have only begun. If present demographic trends are not altered, the populations of most major African cities, already wracked by poverty, will double in a single decade. Whereas today only two African cities (Cairo and Lagos) have more than 5 million residents, in the year 2000 there will likely be eight such giants.

This urbanization is by no means limited to Africa. In 1950, in the entire developing world, only three cities had populations greater than 5 million; by the year 2000, there will be 46 such cities. While only three of those cities had populations greater than 10 million in 1975; by 2000, there will be 21. Most of these cities are today already clogged with the poor, and unemployment rates higher than 25 percent are common. India's urban population, for example, is now 192 million and will grow to 326 million by the end of this century; already, one out of every four of India's city residents lives in a slum.

The population of Dhaka, Bangladesh, as another example, today suffers from 30 percent unemployment and one of the highest population density rates in the world. Yet, its population, 4.9 million in 1985, will swell to perhaps 11.2 million by the year 2000. Even then, there would be 15 other Third World megacities with even larger populations. Mexico City, the largest, would be inhabited by an incredible 26 million people!

"These sizes," reports former World Bank President Robert McNamara, "are such that any economies of location are dwarfed by costs of congestion. The rapid population growth that has produced them will have far outpaced the growth of human and physical infrastructure needed for even moderately efficient economic life and orderly political and social relationships, let alone amenity for their residents."

To make matters worse, virtually all Third World megacities are growing haphazardly, without any urban planning to maximize access to transportation and employment centers; instead, as their populations swell with new births and rural migrants, these cities expand in sprawling, unplanned settlement that maximizes energy inefficiency, consumption, and costs.

Pressures on Societies

Related to the trend toward Third World urbanization is the phenomenon of younger and younger populations. With family size averaging seven or eight children in many parts of the developing world, the Third World is increasingly populated by the young. In Latin America and Asia, nearly 40 percent of the population is under 15 years old; in Africa a full 45 percent is under age 15. This compares with a steady 22 percent in Europe, the United States and Canada.

UNITED NATIONS

In Africa, there are not enough schools

Furthermore, the proportion of youth in Third World populations will continue to grow larger as the 40 percent now under age 15 reach their prime reproductive years. Over the next generation, 3 billion young people will be entering their reproductive years. Even if programs are successful in persuading these groups to have smaller families than their parents had, simple arithmetic dictates that the proportion of population under age 15 may grow much larger.

Educational systems in many developing nations are already strained, making it almost certain that governments will be unable to expand these systems to keep pace with the growing numbers of school-age children. In Nigeria and Kenya, for example, government investments in education are already substantial for developing economies. Even so, schools are being filled beyond capacity and continued growth of the school-age population is outstripping the ability of the governments to build new facilities and train new teachers. As McNamara pointed out, when the school-age population of Latin America grew sharply between 1970 and 1978, "public spending per primary school student fell by 45 percent in real terms."

In Africa, the situation is, if anything, worse. Nigeria's population planning director, Dr. Benson Morah, recently described the situation: "You have schools with 70 children in the classrooms, there are children sitting in the windows, children carrying their chairs to school."

In Kenya, the demographic trends are at least as foreboding. President Daniel Arap Moi has written, "Even if we assume a decline in both fertility and mortality, children aged five years for whom primary school places are needed within one year are expected to increase from about 0.6 million in 1980 to well over 1 million by the year 2000. Under the eight-year primary school system, those aged 6-14 years are expected to increase from about 4 million in 1980 to 8.9 million by the year 2000. Those seeking entry to tertiary institutions (17-18 years) are expected to increase from 1.6 million in 1980 to 3.4 million in the year 2000. The severe pressures that these numbers will exert on physical facilities and teacher requirements will be staggering."

UNITED NATIONS

Kenya's school-age population is booming
□□□□□

If Nigeria and Kenya, whose governments are considered prosperous by African standards, are already falling behind in the provision of education, the outlook is dim for less developed nations as the numbers of children increase dramatically in the near future.

Declines in the quality of education in the Third World are especially disturbing because they portend retreat in the struggle for economic development. Developing nations will be losing ground in the effort to produce educated and capable engineers, scientists, doctors, and civil servants at the very time when they are needed most to lead their nations out of economic stagnation.

The swelling youth population will place enormous new demands not only on schools, but also on the job market, housing, transportation, and basic government social and health services. To continue with Kenya's example, that country's pool of potential workers (measured in Kenya as the population aged 15-49) will more than double by the year 2000, expanding from 6.8 million in 1980 to at least 15.7 million and requiring more than a two-fold increase in the number of available jobs.

Throughout the Southern Hemisphere, the developing nations will have to generate approximately 800 million new jobs in the next 13 years just to accommodate people already born who will be entering the workforce. India alone will have 120 million new people entering its labor pool during that period. Mexico's labor force, in which unemployment is already upwards of 26 percent, is projected to double during the next two decades. To provide jobs for that number of people would require Mexico to create 1 million new jobs each year for the next 20 years; that challenge comes as Mexico, with recent annual economic growth in the quite respectable range of 6 percent, has been able to generate only about 300,000 new jobs each year.

Decline and Destabilization: Characteristics of Present Growth
□

As population growth overwhelms the capacity of developing economies to provide jobs and services, these trends will result in huge urban centers filled with youth who are idle, uneducated and poor, with little reasonable hope for the future. That would certainly exacerbate social splintering and ethnic tensions that already exist in many Third World nations, and would contribute to increased political instability.

Mexico must create 1 million jobs every year
□□□□□

Furthermore, because of this effect, McNamara has called rapid population growth "a major contributor" to the emerging trend toward authoritarian governments in the Third World, as weak governments respond with repression to the rising discontent among their peoples.

Pressures on Human Health

Family planning has clearly demonstrated benefits for human health, just as excessive population growth has the indisputable effect of undermining public health.

To begin with, childbirth itself can be a life-threatening experience, much more so in countries with inadequate health care services. Multiple pregnancies place an even greater strain on the health of women. Studies have documented the link between birth spacing and a decline in infant and maternal mortality. When couples can be educated about how to allow more time between the birth of each child, the chances of survival for each child and for the mother are dramatically improved.

In Tunisia, Syria, Jordan, and Yemen, as examples, infants born less than two years apart are about two and a half times more likely to die in their first year than children born two years apart. The odds of survival improve even more if there is a four-year interval between births. This pattern was present in all 41 developing countries included in the World Fertility Survey, a massive social research project conducted by the International Statistical Institute and principally funded by the United Nations Fund for Population Activities and the United States. That consistency suggests that as many as half of the 15 million infants who die each year in the Third World could be saved through better child-spacing made possible by family planning.

The cycle of rapid successive pregnancies and declining health is wrenching. When pregnancies are repeated in very short intervals, allowing little or no time for recuperation, maternal strength declines. Maternal health and nutrition are believed to be the chief determinants of infant birthweight. Low birthweight, in turn, is the major cause of infant deaths during the first 28 days of life, according to physicians working in the Third World.

UNITED NATIONS

Mothers in Mali seek treatment for their malnourished children

Even for those children who do survive the first critical months, life chances may be dim. One out of every three low-birthweight children suffers brain damage and delayed motor development; more than half will have impaired intelligence. In nations where survival itself is a challenge, such impairment can be fatal. In India, 30 percent of the 25 million babies born each year have low birthweights. That statistic underlies an even more tragic figure: 43 percent of all deaths in India are attributable to children under the age of four.

In addition, by enabling couples to prevent unwanted pregnancies, family planning also helps to prevent abortions and all of their associated health risks. A Columbia University study has estimated that 1,400 women die every day because of complications from pregnancy and abortion, many of which might not have been necessary had family planning been successfully employed.

The example of Brazil is illustrative. Until relatively recently, the Brazilian government did not promote family planning because of the opposition of the Catholic Church and the military. Not coincidentally, the number of unwanted pregnancies was high and many women turned to the prospect of illegal abortions. Consequently, fully 40 percent of the government's public health budget for obstetrical and gynecological services went toward caring for women injured in self-inflicted or "back-alley" abortion procedures.

Overpopulation has a less direct impact on public health as well. By undermining economic development and helping to keep large populations in poverty, overpopulation impedes the delivery of health care in developing nations, particularly to rural areas. In crowded urban centers, public sanitation efforts are undercut by the proliferation of shantytowns established by migrants from rural areas. With poor sanitation, these areas breed disease and early death for many.

Pressures on Ecologies

Perhaps the most obvious impact that growing population has on the environment is the depletion of fixed natural resources. When population increases significantly in a given area, there will naturally be greater demand on fixed natural resources, such as oil, coal, and certain minerals. This also, of course, results in greater pollution and destruction of other fixed and atmospheric resources, such as the ozone layer.

Perhaps less obvious, but equally certain, is the impact of overpopulation on renewable resource systems, such as forests, water, and soil. All such resources have "carrying capacities"—that is, the level at which they can provide maximum yields without injuring their ability to repeat that yield. Just as one can only withdraw so much money from an interest-bearing fund without dipping into the capital, so can one only chop down a certain number of trees in a forest each year without injuring its ability to replace those trees. Carrying capacities can sometimes be enlarged through technological advances, but when population advances faster than technology, carrying capacities are eroded.

UNITED NATIONS

Fresh water is already scarce in Nepal
□ □ □ □ □

Populations in many parts of the developing world have grown so large that they are beginning to exceed the "carrying capacities" of their environments. This is of crucial concern because the economic development of these nations depends largely upon the integrity of their natural resources. If the damage to local environments which results from overpopulation becomes too great, it will jeopardize that population's chances of ever achieving economic self-sufficiency.

The examples of populations exceeding environmental carrying capacities around the world are disturbingly numerous. In Africa, where the chief source of fuel for warmth and cooking is wood, populations survived for centuries off deadwood and renewable scrubwood. Because the populations needed only as much as could be grown anew each year, there was a constant supply of wood available for human use. In recent years, however, growing populations have caused the demand for fuelwood to exceed renewable resources. In Tanzania, for example, according to World Bank figures, a typical household devotes between 250 and 300 working days each year simply to finding and collecting the wood it needs for fuel. The excessive demand has resulted in the taking of wood from sources which are slower to replace themselves.

The unmet need for fuel has also caused some African and Asian populations to burn animal dung that was once used to fertilize the soil. Thus, the damage to one ecology—that of the forests and scrubtrees—has led to the injury of another—the fertility of the soil.

UNITED NATIONS

Desertification: Africa is losing ground

These two trends have combined to create a far more fundamental environmental impact as well. The loss of tree and vegetation cover, when it occurs on a grand enough scale, can affect the cycle of rain and water recovery. Without the vegetation to help absorb and retain moisture, the eventual recycling of water through transpiration, evaporation and new precipitation is crippled. Thus, ecologists have found that in parts of Asia, Latin America, and Africa where there has been rapid deforestation, there has also followed a decline in rainfall. This, in turn, affects the capacity to grow new vegetation cover.

The sandy and unstable soil of the African Sahel, for instance, once deprived of vegetation cover, is particularly vulnerable to erosion. Consequently, in an area where agricultural fertility is already weak, thousands of tons of topsoil and nutrients are washed away each year into the sea. On the global scale, 25 billion tons of arable topsoil vanish from the world's cropland every year.

These factors—the reduction of soil fertility, the loss of ground cover, reduction in precipitation, and soil erosion—have combined to cause the expansion of the vast deserts of the Sahel. The great deserts there have been slowly expanding in recent years, converting what were once acres of arable land into desert. A vivid example of this impact can be seen in Ethiopia. In 1900, 40 percent of Ethiopia was covered by trees and brush. The taking of this tree cover for fuelwood, however, has been so widespread that less than 4 percent of the country now has forest cover. The resulting encroachment of deserts—

called desertification—is measured each year in miles.

Neither the persistent droughts in the Sahel, nor its devastating impact in the recent Ethiopian famine are solely the results of overpopulation. There is strong evidence that the Sahel region is subject to a cyclical environmental pattern in which decade-long droughts occur about every 30 years. At the same time, however, many ecologists believe that the period of drought that precipitated Ethiopia's devastating famine lasted longer than usual because normal weather cycles were compounded by the effects of deforestation.

Similarly, the Ethiopian famine itself is partly the result of misguided government policies that reduced agricultural productivity and hindered the ability of farmers to adjust to drought conditions. And yet it is also clear that coincident booming population growth seriously exacerbated those problems.

Population growth has upset the environmental balance of other parts of the world as well. In Indonesia, the government's population relocation program promoted the rapid settlement of formerly unpopulated parts of Borneo. As the new population cleared large areas of Borneo's rainforests for settlement and fuel, there followed a decline in rainfall and an eventual drying-up of swampland in the region. In early 1983, a subsequent fire, perhaps started when lightening struck dried timber, raged for several months, destroying 3.5 million hectares of forest, and causing vast ecological destruction. Ecologists have estimated that it could take 700 years to restore the area's indigenous rainforests, if indeed they can ever be replaced.

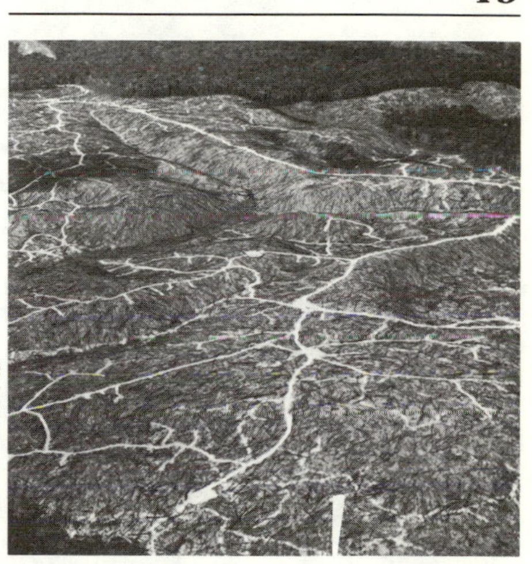

WORLD WILDLIFE FUND

Brazil's rainforests are disappearing
□ □ □ □ □

Worldwide, the destruction of rainforests represents a serious threat to the world's biological diversity and the stability of the carbon cycle. Twenty-seven million acres of rainforests (about the same size as would cover the entire state of Pennsylvania) are lost each year, spurred by disruptions to ecological cycles, by the search for new farmland and fuelwood, and by the temptation to harvest the forests' timber as a quick, but not readily replaceable cash crop.

Three countries—Indonesia, Brazil, and Zaire—contain half the world's rainforests within their borders, and yet none of the three has developed a comprehensive strategy to reverse the loss of the forests.

This loss is significant because the tropical rainforests, while comprising just 7 percent of the world's land area, are home to perhaps 40 percent of the earth's plant and animal species. As a result, with upwards of 2 million species, these lush, intricate forests serve as a vitally important "genetic bank" for future life. Scientists are only beginning to understand the full value and potential of genetic diversity, but already have discovered some highly promising applications in new strains of crops and animals resistant to parasites and disease. These advances, which could revolutionize agricultural productivity and medical science, are possible because of the richness of biological diversity on earth. If the world continues to destroy its precious rainforests—wiping out 40 percent of the planet's genetic diversity along with them—we may never know the lost potential. Already, the world is losing several plant and animal species each day to extinction; within 13 years, the world will likely be losing several hundred species with each passing day. The earth's tropical rainforests could be extinguished as soon as 60 years from now if deforestation continues apace.

WORLD WILDLIFE FUND

Rainforests are valuable as a cash crop, but invaluable as an ecological resource

Pressures on Economies

One population can supplement its financial well-being by harvesting excessive yields—whether it is in the taking of rainforests, fuelwood, or animal life. In doing so, however, it will make repeating the harvest impossible and essentially robs the next generation of full or perhaps any use of that resource. When one generation enhances its income in this way at the cost of the next, it is truly a false economy. When an economy grows beyond its present physical scale, it may increase costs faster than benefits, and initiate an era of uneconomic growth which impoverishes rather than enriches.

The related developments of declining soil fertility, desertification, and changes in rainfall have caused agricultural productivity to decline in a number of Third World nations. Africa used to be an exporter of grain to the rest of the globe. Now, in virtually every African nation, per capita agricultural productivity and per capita income have fallen consistently over the past 10 years. These nations are losing ground in the struggle for economic development.

In one year alone, for example, from 1986 to 1987, Kenya's per capita Gross National Product fell 15 percent. Despite the return of the rains to Ethiopia and a rebound of agriculture, that country's per capita GNP slid 8 percent during a "good year." Zambia's per capita

GNP plunged 31 percent during just that same short, one-year period.

Decline and Destabilization: Characteristics of Present Growth

And while African population grows by 3 percent each year, the continent's food supply increases by only 1 percent. The obvious result of that difference is that each African's share of the continent's food supply is getting smaller and smaller. Over the past 10 years, food production per person in Africa has fallen by 11 percent. The World-watch Institute has charted the divergence in grain production per capita in Western Europe and Africa. The contrast is vivid. In 1950, Western Europeans produced 234 kilograms of grain per capita, while Africans produced 157 kilograms per person. After 35 years, as Europe's population stabilized and Africa's ballooned, production diverged dramatically; Africa's grain production had lost ground to 150 kilograms per capita, while Western Europe's had soared to 501 kilograms per person.

There are clearly a great many factors that inhibit agricultural development in the Third World. But when the United Nations Food and Agriculture Organization (FAO) assembled a panel of experts representing a wide range of agricultural disciplines and asked them to sort out these myriad factors, rapid population growth quickly emerged as the chief culprit. The FAO panel ranked population growth as the most powerful negative influence on global agricultural development, and called it more damaging than debt-service problems, trade stagnation, interest rates, environmental degradation, or agricultural price policies.

WORLD BANK

Overpopulation helps transform fertile land into deserts.

When prolonged declines in agricultural productivity coincide with consistent increases in population, the unavoidable consequence is increased dependence on foreign sources of food. Egypt is only one of many examples. Politically-charged food subsidies, despite reductions, today eat up more than 14 percent of Egypt's national budget. The United States over the past 10 years has provided Egypt with American wheat and corn worth $2.5 billion. The result is that every third loaf of bread baked in Egypt is made from wheat and corn ground in the United States.

And Egypt is not alone in its difficulties. The FAO predicts that by the year 2000, 29 African nations and 64 worldwide will be unable to feed their populations without importing food. Not surprisingly, at the same time, UNICEF has found that malnutrition is on the rise in 10 nations in Africa and six more in Latin America and the Caribbean.

While undermining a nation's per capita productivity and income, population pressures also make life more expensive for individuals as well. Rapid population growth in general, and rapid Third World urbanization in particular, have sapped natural resources and driven up prices. As growing urban populations have deforested the surrounding countryside in the search for fuelwood, for example, the costs have skyrocketed, draining already short family incomes. A study of fuelwood prices in India published by that country's Centre for Energy, Environment and Technology showed that as cities grew and required ever more of an increasingly scarce resource, the real price of fuelwood climbed 42 percent over eight years. And, while growing demand propels the massive taking of trees from Third World nations, developing countries have no plans or policies for managing forest depletion to ensure maximum sustainable yields.

WORLD BANK

Collecting fuelwood in Burkina Faso

Worldwide, only one acre of new trees is planted for every 10 acres of forest cleared. The result is that timberlands equal to 40 Californias will vanish by the end of this century. This loss is both environmentally and economically significant. The Third World as a whole (both industry and families) is dependent on wood for half of its energy needs; Third World families use wood for fully 70 percent of their fuel requirements. Therefore, as the forests disappear, costs are sure to grow even higher, generating a colossal economic burden for developing countries.

Concerns over "food security" and crumbling economies have helped to convince some reticent Third World governments of the need to control population growth.

Oil-producing Nigeria is a timely example. In the 1970s boom years of the Organization of Petroleum Exporting Countries (OPEC), when skyrocketing oil prices were raising Nigeria's per capita income, the government believed it could provide for any sized population and resisted family planning efforts. More recently, however, as oil prices have plunged, taking Nigeria's wealth down with them, the Nigerian government has rethought its policy. Faced with an increasingly enormous population and a seriously weakened economy dependent on food imports, Nigeria in March 1987 embraced one of the continent's most comprehensive and ambitious policies to tame population growth.

One of the most daunting challenges of population growth is its paradoxical relationship with economics. On the one hand, overpopulation has the indisputable effect in the Third World of undercutting economic development and diluting per capita national wealth; at bottom, rapid population growth makes everyone in the population poorer. At the same time, however, there remains an apparent economic incentive for individuals to have more children in the hope that a greater number of offspring will eventually increase the number contributing to family income and to parents' means of support in their old age.

Fertility—defined as the number of children an average woman will have in her lifetime—and standards of living are inextricably linked. The desire for large families is evident in many parts of the Third World. In Mauritania and Senegal, for example, married women report desiring an average of about nine children. This desire is driven largely by the concern of parents to have children who can support them in their old age. When childhood mortality is high and living standards are low, there is an apparent incentive to have more children under the assumption that increasing the number of offspring will increase the chances of financial security in older age.

UNITED NATIONS

Pushing the one-child ideal in China

In this way, rising fertility and declining living standards reinforce each other. With greater numbers of children, per capita income declines. As poverty increases, along with a related increase in infant mortality, it fuels the desire to have more children. In precisely the same way, declining fertility and improving standards of living reinforce each other. Higher living standards diminish the need for parents to have large families. As family size declines, per capita income rises and living standards improve.

These two cycles operate on the family level and on the national level—the first characterized by rapidly increasing population and poverty (as in Africa), and the reverse cycle by stable population and rising economic well-being (as in South Korea and Taiwan). The challenge is how nations can break out of the first cycle and into the second.

Pressures on International Security

The pressures created by rapid population growth on societies, the environment, and national economies can result in conditions that give rise to civil unrest, violence, and international strife. Consider the chief causes of revolution and unrest around the globe today: poverty, hopelessness, political repression, longstanding cultural and ethnic tensions. All of these conditions are aggravated by rapid population growth.

The world has already had its first war caused primarily by the pressures of overpopulation. The 1969 "Soccer War" between El Salvador and Honduras was sparked by Honduran resentment over a growing stream of immigrants from overpopulated El Salvador. With the highest population density of any Central American nation and booming population growth, El Salvador's growing number of disenchanted, unemployed, and impoverished peasants were spilling over into neighboring Honduras, which felt no better equiped to provide for them. There have been many more international conflicts in which population pressures have been a contributing factor if not a primary cause.

Population growth may have its greatest impact on international security through its habit of strangling local economies. Eight hundred million young people will be entering the Third World job market over the next 13 years. With the economies of many developing countries already in decline, many of these young people can expect to remain jobless. Many will migrate to the major cities in their countries, which are very often the national capitals, in search of employment they will never find. Once in the cities, many will settle in appalling squatter camps, where they will look out upon a world divided into the very rich and the very poor, and begin a life of hopelessness and desperation.

UNITED NATIONS

Living conditions threaten children's health in Dhaka

The myriad effects of overpopulation through unemployment, rapid urbanization, environmental degradation, declining public health, and economic stagnation conspire in the Third World to create a potentially explosive threat that can fairly be called the "Aspiration Bomb." This bomb is made up of young people who live in destitute poverty and have little reasonable hope for a better future. At the same time, they are taunted by an awareness of a more affluent world just outside their reach. They see in the streets of their neighborhood wrenching poverty and they see through television and mass media the images of a modern material world.

In a 1980 report on population, the U.S. National Security Council wrote:

> "Recent experience, in Iran and other countries, shows that this younger age group, frequently unemployed and crowded into urban slums, is particularly susceptible to extremism, terrorism, and violence as outlets for frustration. On balance, these

factors add up to a growing potential for social unrest, political instability, mass migrations, and possible international conflicts over control of land and resources. Demographic pressures will certainly reinforce the frustrations caused by absolute and relative poverty. . . . The examples of warfare in recent memory involving India, Pakistan, Bangladesh, El Salvador, Honduras, and Ethiopia, and the growing potential for instability in such places as Turkey, the Philippines, Central America, Iran, and Pakistan surely justify the question (of population pressures) being raised."

Six years later, the security experts of a new administration reached the same conclusion in analyzing the specific causes of terrorism. In its 1986 report, the White House Task Force on Combatting Terrorism, chaired by Vice President George Bush, wrote: "Fully 60 percent of the Third World is under 20 years of age; half are 15 years or less. These population pressures create a volatile mixture of youthful aspirations that when coupled with economic and political frustrations help form a large pool of potential terrorists."

UNITED NATIONS

The "Aspiration Bomb" threatens civil unrest

The "Aspiration Bomb" may well present a greater threat to U.S. security than the atomic bomb. This is because while there is always the hope that mutual deterrence or common sense will preclude the use of nuclear weapons, there is no such counterveiling influence against the violence and frustration embodied in the Aspiration Bomb. If it is not difused by responsible efforts to curb population growth and allow for a better economic future, this threat to U.S. and international security will grow more acute.

In this way, the most pressing challenge to U.S. interests may not lie in the Soviet Union, but in the narrow land stretching from the Rio Grande south to the isthmus of Panama. Political instability, social tensions, and swelling poverty in that region create an Aspiration Bomb ripe for explosion in violence, anger, and revolution. It is no coincidence that the nations of this region also have some of the world's highest fertility rates and fastest growing populations—the region's current population of 118 million would soar to 220 million by the year 2015 at present growth rates. The region can be compared to a pressure-cooker and illegal emigration has always been its safety valve. The new U.S. immigration law holds the potential of closing that valve, thereby adding to the region's tensions.

Costa Rica, a model of democratic stability in this troubled region and an important friend of the United States, has offered a warning. The civil wars which have torn apart Costa Rica's neighbors have resulted in mass migrations of refugees. Their resettlement has combined with rapid population growth and high fertility throughout the region to undermine recent advances in social development and public health. Former Costa Rican President Daniel Oduber Quiros, in Washington during the summer of 1987 to press for U.S. acceptance of Costa Rica's peace plan for Central America, beseeched U.S. policymakers:

"All that we have done in 30 years as far as health is concerned is being destroyed. We had destroyed malaria, and now malaria is back. We had destroyed measles; measles is back. We had destroyed diptheria; now diptheria is back. So our feeling is that no possibility for a solution exists unless you have a cease fire and discuss solutions to the displacement of persons. At the same time, this is the moment when we need more family planning and we need more support from you. We prefer help in family planning and population programs rather than in weapons."

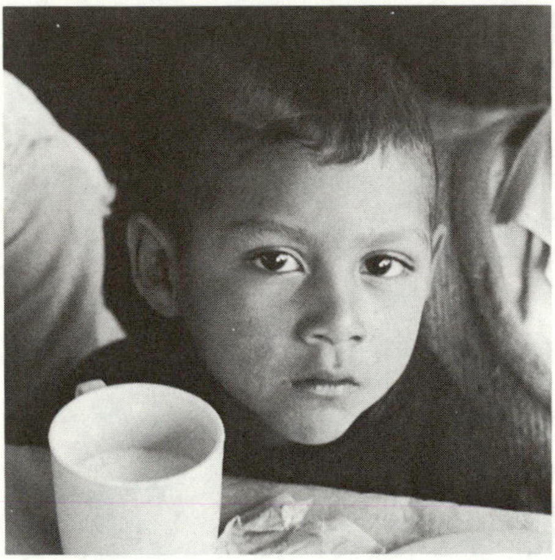

FAO

Nearly half the population of Central America is under 15

Pressures on Industrialized Societies

The damaging effects that rapid population growth can have on U.S. and Western security interests are clear. But overpopulation abroad has other and sometimes more immediate effects as well for North Americans and Europeans.

The National Security Council report cited earlier touched on one of those impacts: "The near certainty of at least a doubling of the populations of most developing countries within the next two to three decades has particular significance for the United States, which has been the goal of so many of the world's emigrants and refugees."

Mounting population pressures in the Third World are sure to fuel the fires of illegal immigration to the United States and other affluent nations. The geographic borders of the United States have already become semi-permeable membranes for illegal aliens. Even if the new U.S. immigration law succeeds in closing the American job market to many of these immigrants through employer sanctions, unemployment and poverty in the United States may seem preferable to unemployment and poverty in the Third World.

Even if overpopulation does not boost American unemployment through illegal immigration and more competition for jobs at home, it will do so by luring American jobs to the Third World. American corporate executives will be hard-pressed to resist the temptation to capitalize on huge labor surpluses in the developing world. Already the shift is underway.

Mexico passed a law in 1983 to entice U.S. corporations. It provided that foreign companies that move operations into Mexico for processing raw materials brought in from abroad would be exempted from having to pay taxes, health benefits, unemployment compensation, and the like. This plan—called the Maquiladores or "twin-plants" concept—has grown by 50 percent in the past four years. It has lured 900 U.S. corporations into Mexico (including 150 in 1986 alone) and has become the country's second greatest source of foreign exchange after oil.

WORLD BANK

Third World hunger will affect affluent societies too

Americans and the residents of other industrialized nations may feel isolated from Third World overpopulation by the relative affluence and security of their modernized societies. It is true that overpopulation will take its most immediate and devastating toll at its source: in developing countries. But the spillover effects will reshape the world economy and the affluence and stability now enjoyed by the industrialized world.

Recent Progress

There have been some encouraging developments in the past two decades. Fertility and population growth rates in a number of countries have declined. In the industrialized world, they have nearly leveled off.

In the developing world, there have also been a few success stories. Thailand, South Korea, Taiwan, and Colombia have all had remarkable success in curbing population growth through committed and well-managed programs to promote voluntary family planning. China's well-publicized program to encourage the one-child family norm has also led to a sharp decline in population expansion. And in a country that accounts for more than 20 percent of total world population, such a decline can have a very important impact on global growth rates.

Even so, there is a long way to go, and there is no assurance that the recent positive trends will continue in the absence of sustained assistance from the industrialized world.

As recently as 25 years ago, virtually the entire Third World viewed continued population growth as desirable and necessary for economic development. Governments believed that more people were needed to settle undeveloped rural areas and bring unused land into productive cultivation. As population skyrocketed, however, under pronatalist government policies, economic productivity began to fall, not rise. As populations strained the ability of governments to provide basic services and as they exceeded carrying capacities and brought on rapid environmental degradation, many of these governments, one by one, began to realize that too-swift population growth would become a hindrance rather than a boon to economic development.

FRANK PRICE

A health worker explains contraceptive options to an Indian mother of nine

□ □ □ □ □

The former military government in Brazil, for instance, long held the view that population growth was needed to settle inland jungles and realize the government's goal of building the largest and most powerful army in Latin America. After years of rapid population growth, what Brazil found, however, was not cultivated jungles but vastly overcrowded coastal cities and quickly spreading poverty. The government's plans for a larger army were also undercut when it found most of the potential recruits unfit for military service because of ill health, childhood malnutrition, or grossly inadequate education. This discovery led to new government policies promoting more responsible population growth.

A growing number of Third World governments have arrived at the realization that economic development is not possible without more stable population growth. Some of these governments, like Bangladesh, have declared the reduction of population expansion to be the nation's first priority. The importance of this transformation in outlook for the Third World toward population planning cannot be overestimated. In Bucharest in 1974, at the first major international conference held to discuss rapid world population growth, it was the nations of the industrialized world that sounded the alarm that overpopulation threatened economic development. Delegates from North America and Europe pressed for the recognition of the relationship between population and development, while most Third World delegates reacted with skepticism. Some suspected racist motivations for American and European calls for limits to African and Asian fertility.

Ten years later, however, when the nations reconvened in Mexico City for the second U.N. International Conference on Population, it was the nations of the Third World that sounded the alarm. Having seen the increasingly vivid impact of rapid population growth in their countries, the Third World delegates led the conference in pressing for a more coherent international response.

The emergence in the Third World of a recognition of the problem and a commitment to work toward solutions has made possible the recent progress that some developing nations have made in curbing fertility. Now one of the greatest uncertainties is whether the United States and other industrialized nations will stand by their original commitments to help.

UNITED NATIONS

In Brazil, there are 10 million abandoned children

There are a great many ways to reduce fertility and population growth. Obviously, family planning can directly reduce a nation's birth rate. Extending the availability of contraceptives is the single most effective way of reducing fertility. In addition, research and development of more convenient, cheaper, and more effective contraceptives can make a difference.

In less direct ways, an elevation in the status of women, delaying age at marriage, wider practice of breastfeeding, reductions in infant mortality, and government social security programs can each contribute to slower population growth.

Given the present rate of growth and the enormous population momentum that already exists, a significant reduction in population expansion will require the successful employment of several of these approaches. At this point, no one by itself will be sufficient.

FACTORS AFFECTING FERTILITY

The good news, however, is that the most easily accomplished and effective among these options—the extension of family planning programs—really works. Financial investments in programs that encourage the use and increase the availability of family planning services yield direct positive results in reducing population growth.

In developing countries with effective family planning programs, fertility declined an average of 30 percent between 1965 and 1975—compared with roughly 4 percent in countries with weak or ineffective family planning efforts and 2 percent in countries without any program.

Successful family planning programs consist of two basic elements: first, efforts to encourage couples to desire smaller families and, second, efforts to increase the availability and effectiveness of contraceptive methods. At bottom, no progress in reducing population growth can be made without three fundamental ingredients: the availability of contraceptives, motivation to use them, and the political will to encourage both.

While it is very true that over 400 million people in the developing world want to limit the size of their families but lack the birth control or knowledge of family planning to do so, it is also true that some Third World couples continue to desire large families.

These couples have desired large families for several reasons. First, in societies in which the status of women is not considered equal to men's, women are often denied options other than bearing and raising children. Second, and perhaps most important, a concern is shared by some Third World couples for raising a sufficient number of children who can later support them in their old age. In the largely agrarian societies of the developing world, there can be an additional motivation because children can double as farm laborers. And, finally, there are sometimes cultural factors that create a form of peer pressure to bear children.

Zimbabwe provides a common example. "Zimbabwean women," explains Sally Mugabe, wife of Prime Minister Robert Mugabe, "live within the context of a local culture that views procreation and reproduction in metaphysical terms. Every person is considered to be spiritually impure and is not permitted to participate in spiritual affairs until after siring or bearing offspring. . . . For a woman, bearing and rearing children is the primary source of her status in the family and the community. The larger the number of children a woman has, the higher the status she enjoys. Some communities perform elaborate ceremonies to honor women on bearing their tenth child."

UNITED NATIONS

Mothers listen to a family planning speaker in Sierra Leone
□ □ □ □ □

In addition to overcoming these motivations to have more children, family planning programs sometimes must also counter negative feelings about birth control rooted in misunderstandings about how contraception works. In Kenya, for example, efforts to promote family planning have been hampered by a succession of rumors about erroneous side-effects and suggestions that the government was secretly trying to sterilize unsuspecting children and adults through chemical additives to food products. Each new rumor means another setback for the government's efforts and makes delivery of family planning services more expensive.

Education About Family Planning

The most effective strategy for overcoming these sorts of problems is education. It must be demonstrated to couples that having very large families diminishes the income available for each child. And that must be backed up by programs that provide couples with some assurance of financial security in their old age. Dispensing contraceptives without providing information about their use and benefits will always be of limited success.

The full range of family planning options—from abstinence and rhythm to the pill and sterilization—must be explained to prospective users. Successful government programs in Thailand, Indonesia, and other parts of the world have found that once couples understand exactly how contraception works, its benefits, and its potential drawbacks, their initial suspicions are dispelled and they can make informed choices to suit their situations. In fact, they often become enthusiastic about the promise family planning holds for a smaller, healthier, and more financially secure family.

Developing country governments, often in cooperation with international donor agencies, have devised and tested a variety of ways to extend this education to their peoples. Indonesia has been successful in spreading knowledge of family planning through many of its Outer Islands by employing a network of local counselors. The Indonesian government has educated representatives from hundreds of rural villages and trained them to provide basic family planning services and information. These representatives, most of whom are women, then return to their native villages to educate other couples about birth control, often going door-to-door to visit with local women and discuss family planning options.

UNITED NATIONS

Indian women learn contraceptive options
□ □ □ □ □

Using a somewhat different approach, the Mexican government has made inroads with its population through its comprehensive "social marketing" campaign to promote the value of smaller families and delaying pregnancy. Like Indonesia and other nations, Mexico has spread its message through advertisements on billboards, radio, and television. But it has gone even further by using T-shirts and producing a popular love song in which a teenage duet agrees to delay having sex.

Mexico also gets credit for the world's first television series designed to promote desire for smaller families and the idea that true "machismo" is proven not through a man's prolific reproduction but by fathering only as many children as he can support. During the nine months that Mexico's family planning "soap opera" was on the air, from August 1977 through April 1978, more than 500,000 Mexican women began planning their families for the first time—an increase of 32 percent over the preceding 12 months.

The government of Kenya has picked up where Mexico left off. In mid-1987, Kenya began broadcasting its own "soap opera." Similar to Mexico's experiment, only tamer in its plot, the Kenyan program is called "Tushauriane" in Swahili, or "Let's Discuss It." The characters and plot line are designed to convey information about the health risks of frequent pregnancy and the benefits of smaller families. The Kenyan government is broadcasting its program on radio in addition to television because Kenyans, 80 percent of whom are rural dwellers, have limited access to television.

Both Mexico and Kenya designed the characters, situations, and dilemmas presented in the "soap operas" to be consistent with the viewers' own life experiences. In this way, viewers were more likely to identify with the programs' essential points because it has been found that all successful population and family planning programs are directly suited to the local clientele being served. If they are to work, any new programs contemplated by international donor agencies must be consistent with local culture and values.

W. LAWSON JONES

Indian billboard: "One Girl is Okay"

Through programs like those in Mexico, Kenya, and Indonesia, some governments in the developing world have achieved distinct gains toward fostering a desire for smaller families and popular acceptance of family planning. In Thailand, for example, women surveyed in 1969 said they desired, on average, 3.8 children; by 1979, that figure had declined to 3.3, and by 1981, the "ideal" family size had fallen to 2.9. (Significantly, for Thai women younger than 25, that figure was even smaller, at 2.5.)

In some other countries, however, in which such programs have not yet been undertaken, a preference for larger families remains entrenched. In Pakistan, for instance, most couples desire about four children (although family size is actually much larger). And in many African nations, including Senegal, Cameroon, Nigeria, Mauritania, and the Ivory Coast, the average couple considers the "ideal" family size to be upwards of eight children. These figures, in contrast to Thailand's, suggest both the effectiveness of education programs and the still-acute need for them in much of the developing world.

Age at Marriage

Social-marketing programs can influence not only perceptions of "ideal" family size, but also of the "ideal" age at which to begin sexual activity and marriage. It is too early to know how successful

Mexico's program aimed at persuading teenagers to postpone becoming sexually active will be. There is a somewhat longer record to consider, however, in government efforts to raise the average age at first marriage. A number of Third World nations in recent years have enacted their first laws setting a minimum age for marriage. In doing so, these countries have somewhat reduced early teenage fertility and, by postponing the birth of a woman's first child, have led to smaller average family sizes.

Beyond legislative efforts, however, the World Fertility Survey found that the two greatest factors influencing age at first marriage were employment and educational opportunities for young women.

The Survey found that in developing nations that had extended primary education for teenage girls, the average age at first marriage increased. By the same token, societies expanding employment opportunities for young women also experienced rising ages at first marriage. Conversely, the Survey found that in societies without enlarged educational and employment opportunities for girls and women, females continued to marry at very young ages.

FAO

When women delay marriage, they typically have fewer children

Overall, countries with high population growth rates continued to have low average ages at marriage, whereas countries with more successful population programs had experienced significant increases in such averages.

In Bangladesh, for example, most girls have become brides by age 13 (this is actually slightly higher than a few decades ago). In South Korea, on the other hand, where population is being brought into a more manageable growth pattern, the average age at first marriage has risen from 17.8 several decades ago to roughly 23 today.

Promoting Opportunities for Women

In societies in which women are confined to the roles of wife and mother, there is also typically high fertility. The nations of Africa and the Middle East stand out as examples.

On the other hand, in societies in which women are accepted in the work-force and there are alternatives to child-bearing, fertility usually declines. This has been the case with the industrialized nations of the Northern Hemisphere, and in developing countries such as Brazil, Mexico, Thailand, and South Korea.

In addition, sex discrimination in education and employment is almost always matched by discrimination in the home. In societies which deny women equal rights, women are also often denied an equal say in family decisions concerning family planning, pregnancy, and child-raising. Since it is women who bear the burden of pregnancy, its attendant health risks, and the primary burden of child-rearing, it is reasonable to believe that if given a fuller choice, some women might choose to delay or avoid future pregnancies. In this way also, promoting the status and rights of women could lead to a reduction in fertility.

The relationship between the status of women and fertility is much like that between population growth and impaired economic development: It is not always clear which phenomenon causes the other, nor can it usually be scientifically documented, but the two are almost always seen as a pair. Progress or decline in one category almost universally is seen in concert, respectively, with progress or decline in the other. Thus, in nations with declining fertility, there are almost always tangible improvements in the status and opportunities for women, and vice versa. This connection can even be seen within nations: India's government, for example, has charted regional correlations linking high fertility with low female literacy and early marriage.

FAO

Women learn to write in Benin
□ □ □ □ □

In recognition of this relationship, many nations have integrated into their population-control efforts programs to promote education and employment opportunities for women. Current statistics, however, demonstrate how far we have to go: women still do two-thirds of the world's work, but earn only 10 percent of its income and own less than one percent of its property.

Infant Mortality

Some couples in the Third World's impoverished countries feel pressure to have a sufficient number of children to help provide family income and security in the parents' old age. In many of these countries, medical and social conditions are such that many children will die before reaching their first birthdays. Many others will die later in childhood. The United Nations Children's Fund (UNICEF) reports that in eight African countries (Mali, Sierra Leone, Gambia, Malawi, Guinea, Ethiopia, Somalia, and Mozambique), every fourth child will die before reaching his or her fifth birthday.

Many of these infant deaths are caused because poor couples do not have access to family planning or do not realize the importance of planning proper child-spacing. The Executive Board of UNICEF in 1987 set as its goal cutting global infant and child mortality rates in half by the year 2000. Appropriately, in its plan for meeting that goal, the UNICEF board included efforts to extend family planning along with child immunization and nutrition programs. Moreover, UNICEF Executive Director James Grant has called family planning "one of the most important single steps which can now be taken toward reducing infant mortality and increasing the health of both mothers and children."

Given the high incidence of early death, however, parents may perceive an incentive to have more children than they actually desire, in order to insure against the possible loss of one or more of their children before adulthood.

It has been argued by some that if parents can be given a satisfactory assurance that all of their children will survive and reach adulthood, they will be more inclined to limit the number of their pregnancies.

So, while it may seem intuitive that a reduction in the infant death rate ought to contribute to population growth, it may actually promote an eventual and permanent decline in fertility. This explains why organizations dedicated to reducing population growth are concerned not only with bringing down birth rates, but also with lowering infant and maternal death rates. It explains, too, why organizations dedicated primarily to the welfare of children also recognize the importance of promoting family planning and proper child-spacing, programs most often championed by population organizations. The two goals—population stabilization and maternal and child welfare—go hand in hand. Reducing infant and child mortality is a humanitarian imperative, but it is also a means of stabilizing population growth over the long term.

UNITED NATIONS

Children provide family labor
□ □ □ □ □

Breastfeeding

Programs promoting breastfeeding also help to reduce fertility in two ways. The first and most direct way is that when a woman breastfeeds her child, it delays the return of ovulation following pregnancy, in some cases for as long as a year. While breastfeeding is an unreliable contraceptive method for an individual, it can prevent or delay a successive pregnancy for some months following a birth and can reduce overall fertility.

As a secondary impact, breastfeeding also can influence fertility by reducing infant mortality. By delaying second pregnancies, breastfeeding contributes to better child-spacing, which, in turn, greatly improves each child's life-chances. Also, breastfeeding often improves a newborn's nutritional intake over alternative methods of feeding. This two-fold influence brings down infant mortality, reducing long-term fertility.

In addition to reducing fertility, breastfeeding can ultimately lower maternal mortality through its contributions to better child-spacing. Just as proper child-spacing helps save the lives of children, it also has the benefit of improving the mother's chances of surviving pregnancy and childbirth. A 1981 Columbia University study showed that a mother's survival chances increase significantly if she waits two years between pregnancies.

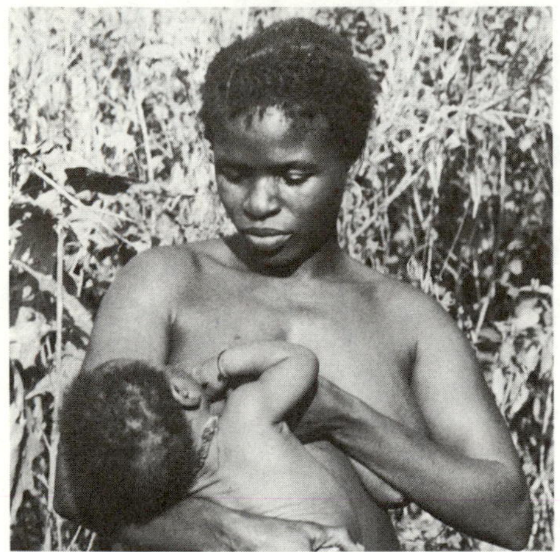

FAO

Breastfeeding contributes to better child-spacing and better maternal and child health

A good measure of how the world is doing in its struggle to control its population growth can be found by taking a closer look at 20 fast-growing developing nations. These 20 countries account for fully 69 percent of present world population growth. Therefore, their success in limiting their individual growth will largely determine how successful the world will be at curbing overall population growth.

Following the name of each country in this section, figures are given for that country's population in 1990, its projected population in the year 2000, and the number of years it would take each country to double its population at current growth rates.

A CLOSER LOOK AT 20 NATIONS

Mexico
Brazil
Egypt
Nigeria
Zaire

A Closer Look At 20 Nations

BANGLADESH

1990 Population: 117.9 m.
2000 Population: 154 m.
Doubling Time: 25 Years

Perhaps no where else in the world are the tragic consequences of overpopulation more vividly apparent than in Bangladesh. In 1950, 43 million people lived in Bangladesh, a country of fertile soil and lush rains. Today, with more than 117 million people living in a land only slightly larger than the State of Louisiana, Bangladesh's population is overrunning its once productive croplands and is gripped by terrible poverty.

W. LAWSON JONES

President Ershad explains Bangladesh's policy to the author

The government of Bangladesh has recognized continuing population growth as "the nation's number one problem and its principal obstacle to socio-economic development." The government has demonstrated a genuinely strong commitment to reducing population growth and has set as its goal achieving replacement level fertility (that is, an average of two children per couple) by the year 2000.

Despite the government's commitment, however, and despite a government program dating back 25 years to promote family planning, Bangladesh has enjoyed little success in curbing population growth. After two decades of effort, knowledge of family planning techniques among the Bangladeshi population is quite high—in fact, 98 percent of Bangladeshi couples know of at least one method of birth control, and 70 percent know of at least five. In this regard, the government's program has been highly successful.

Also encouraging is that Bangladeshi couples have shown receptivity to family planning efforts and a majority say they want smaller families.

But, while knowledge of and desire for birth control is widespread, the availability of contraceptives and family planning services is not. As a result, scarcely 20 percent of Bangladeshi couples are actually practicing birth control. If Bangladesh is to achieve its goal of replacement fertility by 2000, that figure must rise dramatically, reaching 67 percent in 2000.

New commitments, including substantial new amounts of outside assistance, will be required almost immediately if Bangladesh is to be successful in reducing fertility. The growth momentum is strong, with nearly half the population under age 15 and only beginning to enter its reproductive years. The willingness of the Bangladeshi government to fund and cooperate in efforts to make family planning more widely available is, however, encouraging and an essential ingredient to any successful program.

Bangladesh's population growth rate remains high, at 2.7 percent, although this is down from an all-time high of 3.2 percent in the early 1960s.

BRAZIL

1990 Population: 150.3 m.
2000 Population: 180 m.
Doubling Time: 34 Years

PLANNED PARENTHOOD

Housing in
Rio de Janeiro
□ □ □ □ □

The Brazilian government abandoned its traditional policy encouraging population growth in the late 1970s after the adverse effects of overpopulation on the nation's economy and environment became apparent. In 1980, then-President Joao Baptista Figueiredo acknowledged in his inaugural address: "The success of social development programs depends largely on family planning."

The government, once hesitant to promote family planning because of the opposition of the Catholic Church, the military, and certain nationalists, has recently begun to support such efforts indirectly. Still, however, most services are provided through an effective network of private family planning organizations, and affordable oral contraceptives are widely available without prescription at Brazilian pharmacies. (Ninety percent of oral contraceptive and condom users in Brazil purchase their supplies at privately operated pharmacies.)

Consequently, fertility has fallen in Brazil. Brazilian women now have on average just over three children, down from an average of six children in the 1960s. Sixty-five percent of Brazilian couples now use birth control, and progress continues to be made in extending contraceptive availability to the country's rural areas. In Brazil's largely agrarian Northeastern sector, for example, contraceptive use among married women now stands at 53 percent, up from 37 percent in 1980.

Despite such encouraging trends, however, nearly half of all Brazilian women who had been pregnant in the past five years reported in 1986 that their last pregnancy had been unwanted or unintended.

Interestingly, the opposition to family planning in Brazil has not come only from the Church, but also from the left, apparently in part because some leftist radicals view continued overpopulation, with its incident poverty and destabilizing effects, as an important component of any future revolution.

If Brazil is to achieve replacement level fertility by 2000, a goal the government has endorsed, use of family planning must spread to 74 percent of Brazilian couples. Given the widespread acceptance of family planning in Brazil, and the government's recent efforts to help, this is not an unrealistic goal.

WORLD BANK

Many Burmese children can have little hope for the future unless population growth subsides

BURMA

1990 Population: 41.7 m.
2000 Population: 52 m.
Doubling Time: 30 Years

Burma is nearly as impoverished as its neighbor Bangladesh—its per capita annual income of $190 is only $40 more than Bangladesh's. But because of its larger land area and smaller population, Burma's government has not yet felt the population pressures that Bangladesh now feels so acutely. (Bangladesh's population density of 702 persons per square kilometer, compared with Burma's 55 persons per square kilometer, makes its problem far more unmistakable.)

The absence of such obvious overcrowding in Burma allows the government to maintain a pronatalist policy which discourages family planning as a means of reducing fertility. It is not surprising, therefore, that the growth rate of Burma's population has remained relatively steady at about 2 percent.

While the government does not promote family planning in any way, it does recognize it as a legitimate means of providing longer spacing between births, thereby reducing infant and maternal mortality. Infant mortality has remained high through the 1980s at 70 deaths per 1000 infants.

Burma's growth rate and fertility, while not the highest in the developing world, are not likely to subside unless the government changes its view of population expansion.

CHINA

1990 Population: 1.12 b.
2000 Population: 1.3 b.
Doubling Time: 49 Years

China in recent years has identified rapid population growth as the greatest hindrance to economic growth. It has pressed its controversial goal of the one-child family over the past several years and has achieved a significant reduction in the population growth rate.

In 1980, China raised the minimum legal age of marriage by two years to 22 years of age for men and 20 years for women—although the minimum age is greater in some higher density areas like Beijing, where men must be at least 28 years old and women at least 25 before they may legally marry. Along with raising the legal age of marriage, China also established a number of social and economic incentives for couples to have no more than one child, including income bonuses, promises of higher pensions, priority consideration in urban housing assignments, subsidies in health care, and private vegetable gardens for city residents. For couples who have more than two children, there can also be disincentives, including wage deductions of 10 percent to fund welfare programs.

UNITED NATIONS

For China's only children, life expectations are rising
□ □ □ □ □

Over the past year, however, the Chinese government has begun to re-evaluate its policy somewhat as it has begun to realize its potential effects on community and family structure. If the one-child family policy were actually achieved completely, China would become a society without brothers, sisters, aunts, or uncles. In 1987, after nearly eight years of the one-child family experiment, some fears began to surface about the possibility of an emerging generation of spoiled and self-centered only children. Some Chinese are questioning whether such a generation would be compatible with the outward-oriented ideals of a socialist society.

As the numbers of children drop radically under the policy, China would also find itself with more than 60 percent of its population over the age of 65, increasing substantially the burden on the younger, working population to support the elders.

China is by no means abandoning its one-child family policy, but it has relaxed its assertion somewhat. This relaxation in certain rural areas, combined with an increase in the number of women of childbearing age, resulted in a sizeable upswing in Chinese fertility during the mid-1980s. The 1986 birth rate climbed to 20.77 births per 1000 persons, up from 17.8 only the year before. In the isolated western province of Qinghai, the number of births rose 34 percent during the same year. That translates into an increase in the Chinese population of 14 million in 1986 alone—1.6 million more than planned. Such increases jeopardize China's goal of holding its population to 1.2 billion in the year 2000.

While China has retained government incentives for couples who agree to limit their families to just one child, a 1987 State Department report on human rights concluded that China has improved its implementation of its population policy. China has consistently denied allegations that it has sought to coerce couples into practicing birth control or having abortions, but it has conceded that some excesses may have occurred in local administration of the policy. Concern that China's incentive policy has been uniformly successful or effectively coercive should be tempered by the fact that half of all births in China during 1986 were second or third births; moreover, only 21 percent of Chinese families are one-child families.

UNITED NATIONS

China's young people are delaying marriage

While monitoring should occur to ensure the voluntary nature of the program, donor governments ought to support China's goal of sharply reducing population growth. With 22 percent of the world's population, China's success in limiting its growth will largely determine the world's.

And the need for continued efforts in China is evident. If China had not reduced its birth rate from the 1960 average of six children per family to its current 2.2 children per family, it would be facing a total population of 2 billion by the year 2000. Even more incredible, it would be expecting 5.2 billion people by the year 2025, a number larger than now inhabit the entire planet.

But China's effort to stabilize its population growth has not yet been won. China experienced a sharp increase in the number of births following that country's famine of the early 1960s. The children born during that period are now entering their child-bearing years. We can, therefore, expect some continued increase in the Chinese birth rate, at least over the short term, and the degree to which China relaxes or tightens its one-child policy will likely determine its success in achieving its goal of a 1.2-billion population in the year 2000.

EGYPT

1990 Population: 56.3 m.
2000 Population: 72 m.
Doubling Time: 24 Years

Egypt is one of the five largest recipients of bilateral U.S. aid, but only a very small fraction goes toward family planning efforts. President Hosni Mubarak has acknowledged the importance of curbing population growth in order to achieve economic self-sufficiency, but government programs have not been very effective.

Overall, 24 percent of married Egyptian women use birth control. That rate is somewhat disappointing, given the number of years that a family planning program has been in place. Like that in Bangladesh, the Egyptian program has succeeded in promoting knowledge of family planning—90 percent of married women report knowing of at least one method of birth control. But, as in Bangladesh, actual availability of contraceptives has not kept pace.

UNITED NATIONS

The slums of Cairo are built on garbage
□□□□□

The Egyptian government has adopted the "development approach" to population problems, which is the indirect, mostly passive approach. The government has placed special emphasis on increasing women's participation in the labor force, agricultural modernization, improving social security, and reducing the infant mortality rate. All of these initiatives are laudable and each may eventually affect Egypt's birth rate. If Egypt is serious, however, about achieving its goal of 60-percent contraceptive use by the year 2000, the government will have to emphasize to a greater degree the direct approach as well: family planning.

There is evidence of large unmet demand for family planning in Egypt. Fully half of all couples have said they do not desire another child, and yet with contraceptive use at only 24 percent, many of them can expect unwanted pregnancies.

Strapped with heavy foreign debt, declining agricultural productivity, and growing dependence on foreign sources of food and economic aid, Egypt's economic future depends upon its ability to limit population growth.

Only 4 percent of Egypt's 40,000 square miles is arable; the rest is desert. And 99 percent of the country's population is crowded onto the narrow strips of fertile land bordering the Nile River. If Egypt's population doubles in 24 years, as it would at present growth rates, the ability of that narrow valley to accommodate the new numbers is uncertain.

What is certain is that without the massive U.S. aid it now receives, Egypt's economy would be in grave condition. Given the importance of Egyptian stability to U.S. interests, it is essential that more comprehensive efforts be made to extend the availability and acceptance of family planning.

UNITED NATIONS

Ethiopians face an uncertain future

ETHIOPIA

1990 Population: 50.8 m.
2000 Population: 72 m.
Doubling Time: 33 Years

While the government of Ethiopia considers the country's population growth to be "too high, unsatisfactory," it has no official population policy, nor any program to reduce population growth.

The government has set as its primary population-related objectives the reduction of Ethiopia's infant mortality rate and an improvement in the status of women, goals which, if achieved, could serve to reduce fertility indirectly. Given the country's traumatic social and economic dislocation, however, it is questionable whether progress toward these two goals can be significant and quick enough to have any meaningful impact on the country's population growth.

Very little, if any, of the recent famine relief went toward curbing fertility and separate international efforts to promote family planning in Ethiopia have had very limited impact.

Until Ethiopia's government genuinely appreciates the link between population growth and impeded economic development, and undertakes a program to reduce fertility, Ethiopia's population will continue to grow far faster than the economy's ability to support it. In this event, Ethiopia's status as Africa's third most populous nation could change by surpassing Egypt to become the continent's second most populous, but its status as the world's poorest will probably not.

INDIA

1990 Population: 853.4 m.
2000 Population: 1.05 b.
Doubling Time: 32 Years

India's enormous population would double in just 32 years if present growth is maintained. In that case, India, now the world's second most populous country and growing by 18 million people annually, would very likely surpass China and become the most populous on earth. Already, India's population is larger than the combined populations of the Soviet Union, the United States and Indonesia, the world's third, fourth, and fifth most populous nations.

The toll of India's rapid population growth is startling. While India has effectively capitalized on technological innovations to achieve (for now) agricultural self-sufficiency, that productivity is threatened by the growing population's environmental impacts. According to Indian government statistics, overcultivation is causing the deterioration of 2.5 million hectares of Indian land each year, while overgrazing and deforestation convert 1 million hectares of cropland and pastures and 1.5 million hectares of forestland into wasteland annually. With tree and grass cover gone, India loses 6 billion tons of topsoil every year. Finally, soil erosion has turned 4 million hectares of once-productive Indian land into ravines and contributed to the doubling of India's flood-prone zones. All of these developments put India's food security in jeopardy and, with 250 million Indians now living on land prone to flooding, creates the potential for natural disasters.

UNITED NATIONS

Indian women walk to work. More job opportunities are needed for Third World women
□ □ □ □ □

The Indian government has long recognized population growth as a serious impediment to economic development, but programs to promote family planning have met with uneven and limited success. Part of the problem is that although Prime Minister Rajiv Gandhi seems genuinely committed to curbing population growth, India's unwieldy bureaucracy inhibits the successful administration of programs.

India has had a population control program in place since 1952, making it one of the oldest in the world. After 35 years of government effort, 90 percent of Indian couples report knowing of at least one method of birth control, but only 39 percent actually use one. Given this record of limited success, India's goal of 60-percent contraceptive use by the year 2000 seems ambitious. During that same 13-year period, 140 million Indian girls now below the age of 15 will become potential mothers.

The government recently announced the latest in a series of new programs, but it is too early to know if it will realize greater gains than previous efforts. The government is also exploring the idea of adopting an incentive program in jobs and housing for couples who agree to meet family planning goals. In addition, the government is pushing efforts to raise the average age at marriage, advance female literacy and employment opportunities for women, and decrease infant mortality, all of which could reduce fertility over the long term.

U.S. and United Nations development officials have said India has shown "substantial political will and budget commitments" to improve its record. India, which pays for 90 percent of its own family planning efforts, is spending more than $200 million on population programs.

India's population goals remain ambitious, but the government's demonstrated commitment to new and hopefully more successful family planning programs is encouraging.

UNICEF

Indonesia: Many children must work to support their families
□ □ □ □ □

INDONESIA

1990 Population: 188.3 m.
2000 Population: 223 m.
Doubling Time: 35 Years

Next to Thailand, Indonesia has probably the most successful family planning program in Southeast Asia.

When the government launched its population program in 1970, only 2 percent of Indonesian couples were using any kind of birth control. By 1984, that figure had soared to 58 percent. The result is that the country's birth rate has fallen by a third over roughly the same period.

Indonesia's success is made more remarkable in light of the fact that there exists a significant suspicion among many of the nation's rural dwellers about contraception.

The government has overcome much of this concern through a

broadly based media and information campaign to improve understanding of family planning and to rally popular support for the ideal of the smaller, healthier family. Television and radio advertisements, billboards, and fliers have all trumpeted the theme that "two children are enough." In many villages, church bells ring at a set time each day to remind women to take their birth control pills.

In rural areas, that effort has been buttressed by an extensive grass-roots network of local villagers who go door-to-door to counsel neighbors about family planning. This localized approach is important in a country made up of more than 3,000 individual islands, many of which are remote and not easily accessible.

Indonesia's fertility and population growth rate remain quite high by industrialized Western standards, but considering the distance that Indonesia has traveled since 1970, its progress in curbing growth is satisfactory and the outlook for continued improvement is good.

UNITED NATIONS

Iran: little progress since the revolution

IRAN

1990 Population: 55.7 m.
2000 Population: 76 m.
Doubling Time: 20 Years

Although the Iranian government does not ban private efforts to promote family planning—so long as they are consistent with Islamic law—the government is satisfied with current population growth rates and does not seek a reduction.

International population assistance to Iran has been limited since the 1979 revolution, and the country's primary non-governmental population organization, the Family Planning Association of Iran, has been effectively disbanded by the revolutionary government.

Population growth will continue to be limited by the elevated death rate brought on by the Iran-Iraq War, and the government is unlikely to seek fertility declines as long as the war continues. Despite the war's enormous casualties, Iran's population appears to be growing swiftly, perhaps by as much as 3.4 percent annually. If that estimate were correct, Iran's population would double in size in just 20 years. This pace is unlikely to change unless the government alters its view of population growth.

KENYA

1990 Population: 25.1 m.
2000 Population: 38 m.
Doubling Time: 17 Years

An average Kenyan woman will have eight children, making Kenya's fertility among the highest documented in the world. Kenya's population growth rate, also the highest in the world, is an astonishing 4 percent, which means the country's population doubles in a brief 17 years.

Kenya has long been an oasis of relative political, economic, and social stability in turbulent East Africa. But that stability is increasingly threatened by the pressures brought on by such rapid population growth.

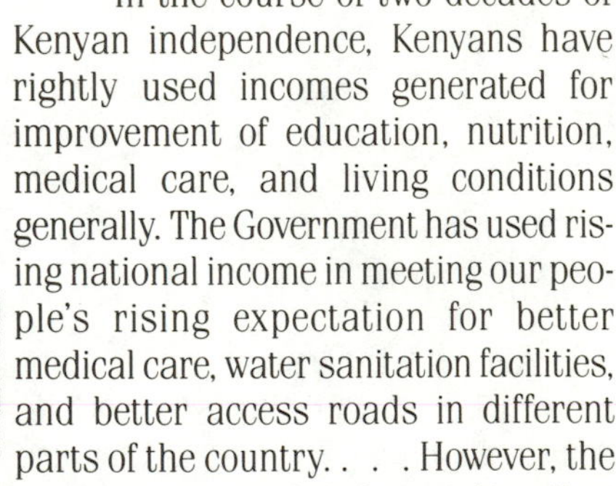

UNITED NATIONS

Kenya: astonishing population growth

President Daniel Arap Moi has warned of this danger:

"In the course of two decades of Kenyan independence, Kenyans have rightly used incomes generated for improvement of education, nutrition, medical care, and living conditions generally. The Government has used rising national income in meeting our people's rising expectation for better medical care, water sanitation facilities, and better access roads in different parts of the country. . . . However, the high rate of population growth and its structural and spatial implications have in turn magnified the development problems that were just incipient at the time of independence. . . . The high rates of population growth threaten the existing levels of living and resource availability as well as provision of social services."

While Kenya's president and vice-president have shown a strong commitment to reducing population growth, the government's efforts have been hampered by a distrust of family planning among some segments of the public. The government has had to dispel fears fueled by rumors that it was sterilizing children through implants in school lunches and that it had secretly tainted Kenyan beer with contraceptive chemicals.

Another obstacle faced by the government has been longstanding rivalries among tribes in Kenya's rural areas. Kenya's population is comprised of more than 70 tribes, twelve of which are major ethnic or political divisions. These tribes are further divided among four broad language groups. Some of these tribes or tribal clusters maintain deep suspicions of other tribes and use tribal populations as a gauge of political strength. The Kenyan government has the challenge of persuading these groups of the benefits of family planning.

The government's latest initiative is the production of radio and television "soap operas" designed to educate Kenyans about the health risks of frequent pregnancy and the benefits of having smaller families. Even if more Kenyans accept the message and desire smaller families, however, a significant hurdle to progress remains the limited availability of family planning services.

The Kenyan government has made some strides in the past several years, but it will take far more resources and time to halt the country's powerful momentum toward population growth. Even if Kenya achieves its first target of slowing population growth from today's 4 percent to 2.8 percent by the year 2000, that would barely bring it into line with the continent's current growth average and would still mean a doubling time of just 25 years.

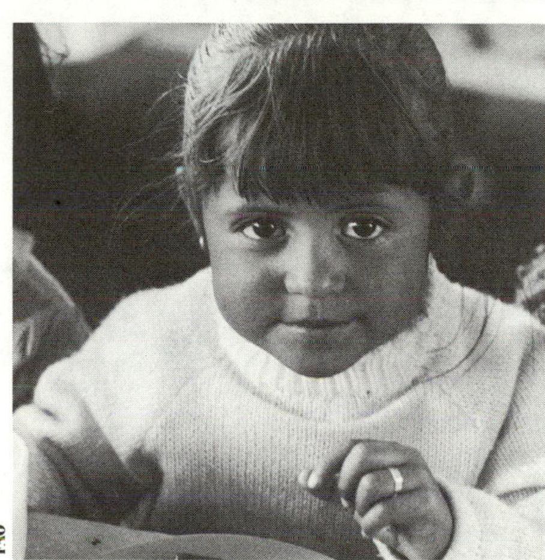

FAO

In Mexico, lower fertility has enabled a better living standard
□□□□□

MEXICO

1990 Population: 88.8 m.
2000 Population: 108 m.
Doubling Time: 29 Years

Mexico's government, like Brazil's, maintained a pronatalist population policy until 1972, when the ill effects of overpopulation became too obvious to misinterpret. Mexico City, the world's most populous urban center, has helped to illustrate those effects vividly with its choking pollution, traffic jams, human congestion, and deepening poverty.

In 1972, the government adopted a program to encourage family planning and reduce fertility, and it has become one of the most successful of its kind. There has been a 20-percent decline in Mexico's birth rate over the past 10 years, and the prevalence of contraceptive use has risen from 12 percent in 1974 to more than 50 percent in 1987. In addition, Mexico has cut infant mortality in half since the 1950s.

Mexico is in the forefront of a family planning strategy in which mass media and entertainment are employed to convey the message that unwanted pregnancies can be prevented. The government has spread this message through broadcasting, posters, T-shirts, and even by recording popular music urging teenagers to postpone sex.

In 1978, Mexico set a preliminary population goal of 2.5 percent annual growth by 1982. It achieved that goal ahead of schedule and has made further progress toward its longer-term goal of 1 percent growth by 2000.

With the recent slide in oil revenues and Mexico's subsequent economic crisis, the government has tried to shield its population program from cutbacks that could erode existing gains. But if the country's economic woes do not abate, some cutbacks seem inevitable, and achievement of the government's population goals could be in jeopardy.

50

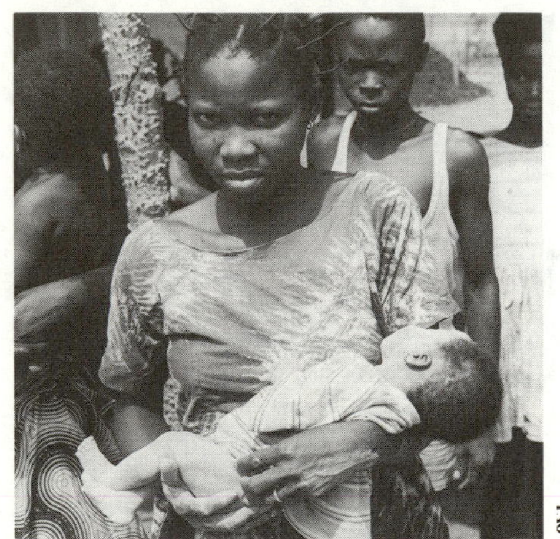

FAO

Nigeria's oil boom-days are over

□ □ □ □ □

NIGERIA

1990 Population: 118.6 m.
2000 Population: 161 m.
Doubling Time: 24 Years

Nigeria, with a very large population and a high 3 percent growth rate, has only begun the task of curbing population growth. In 1931, Nigeria had about 19 million inhabitants. At its present growth rate, Nigeria's now 118 million population would grow to 161 million in 2000 and balloon to an incredible (and impossible) one billion within 75 years!

After years of little action, Nigeria has recently realized the crucial importance of avoiding that crowded future through an ambitious government population policy. Spurred by plummeting oil revenues and increasing dependence on foreign food sources, the Nigerian government in March, 1987, unveiled a $100-million, 5-year plan to curb fertility through wide-ranging family planning efforts.

The plan holds promise and the government's evident new commitment offers important encouragement. There has been some recent progress. The birth rate in Lagos, Nigeria's capital and largest city, was 40 per 1000 persons in 1983, with only two out of 100 women practicing birth control. By 1987, contraceptive use among Nigeria's urban women had crept up to 6 percent and the birth rate had fallen to 30 per thousand. Even so, the population of Lagos and its teeming squatter settlements is booming: the capital now is home to more than 7 million people, up from 329,000 just 35 years ago. With nationwide contraceptive use rates still below 5 percent, Nigeria has a long way to go.

PAKISTAN

1990 Population: 113.6 m.
2000 Population: 146 m.
Doubling Time: 24 Years

Pakistan's experience in population planning demonstrates the importance of dedicated and sustained effort. The Pakistani government recognized early the importance of population control to economic development and in 1965 launched a major family planning program.

That early program succeeded in increasing knowledge of family planning so that in 1975, three out of four married Pakistani women knew of at least one method of birth control. Because the availability of contraceptives remained low, so did actual contraceptive use, rising to only 5.2 percent in 1975. Even so, the program held promise provided family planning services could be expanded to keep pace with knowledge and demand.

UNITED NATIONS

Urban congestion in Lahore, Pakistan

The government suspended its efforts in the late 1970s, however, and when a new survey was conducted between 1979 and 1980 the number of married women who knew of one method of modern birth control had dropped to 25 percent and contraceptive use had slid to 3.3 percent. Thus, the early gains Pakistan made toward taming population growth were nearly erased by a three-year lapse in family planning efforts.

Pakistan has been hard pressed to make up these losses. The government estimates that about 6.6 percent of married women are now using contraceptives, although that figure is probably optimistic. Earlier this decade it had aimed to reduce fertility by 1988 to 5.4 children per woman. Last year, however, fertility remained significantly higher, at 6.7 children, making it extremely improbable that the government will achieve its goal. Pakistan's 1986 birth rate of 42 births per 1000 population also remained far above its 1988 target of 36.2 births.

PHILIPPINES

1990 Population: 66.7 m.
2000 Population: 86 m.
Doubling Time: 25 Years

The Filipino government launched a government population program in 1970 and eventually overtook what until then had been a largely scattered private effort to promote family planning.

The government achieved a reduction in the population growth rate from 3 percent in 1970 to 2.5 percent in the mid-1980s. It accomplished this through the establishment of urban family planning clinics and an outreach program aimed at the 70 percent of Filipinos who live in rural areas.

WORLD BANK

Filipino children crowd a bamboo hut

The government had sought to reduce population growth to 2 percent by 1987, but the rate of growth was actually turning up during that year and some estimates placed it as high as 2.8 percent.

The future of family planning under the new government of Corazon Aquino remains unclear. It is not yet known to what extent the Catholic Church, which helped bring President Aquino to power, will influence the new government's population policy.

There are, however, some troubling indications. The government's family planning commission has been reorganized and placed under the direction of Social Services Minister Mita Pardo de Tavera, who has, in turn, announced that the best way to curb population growth is through economic development. While Minister de Tavera has promised that all forms of birth control will remain available, she has stated her own preference for natural family planning over more modern methods.

Also troubling is a change in the country's constitution. The Philippines was one of the first nations to acknowledge in its constitution the responsibility of government to help extend family planning options to the people. That pioneering provision was removed when the country adopted a new constitution in February 1987.

These developments, coinciding with the recent upswing in the Filipino birth rate, have raised fears that the hard-fought gains made over the past two decades toward lower fertility may be lost. Whether the new government realizes it or not, the resurgence of population growth, with its attendant destabilizing effects on the economy and social structure, will only play into the hands of the rebels who now oppose the government.

The success of President Aquino's democratic revolution is critically important to U.S. security interests in the Pacific. It is clear that continued reductions in fertility and population growth are essential to the new government's efforts to stabilize the country's faltering economy and provide a more prosperous, stable, and democratic future for the Filipino people.

SOUTH KOREA

1990 Population: 43.7 m.
2000 Population: 49 m.
Doubling Time: 53 Years

UNITED NATIONS

Washing clothes

The government has sought to reduce the rate of population growth since the 1960s, and has enjoyed a high rate of success. South Korea's population growth rate has slowed to 1.4 percent and fertility averages 2.1 children per woman.

Also encouraging was the government's adoption in the early 1980s of a more comprehensive growth policy which integrates population and economic development goals.

South Korea appears to have nearly achieved its goal of replacement level fertility (2 children per woman) by the end of this decade. In so doing, it has provided an example for the rest of Asia of the interrelationship between population and economic development. There are many factors that account for South Korea's rising economic fortunes and spreading modernization, but the country's success in curbing rapid population growth has made the convergence of factors possible.

TANZANIA

1990 Population: 27.2 m.
2000 Population: 40 m.
Doubling Time: 19 Years

The Tanzanian government began to recognize earlier this decade the implications of continued population growth. The government maintains, however, that the best way to reduce population growth is through an improvement in the standard of living and economic development.

Former Tanzanian President Julius Nyerere strongly advocated the benefits of family planning and child-spacing. But there is now a new government and, despite some hopeful signs, it has not yet initiated any serious effort to curb fertility.

UNITED NATIONS

A Thai child cares for her siblings

At the same time, one estimate of infant mortality (one determinant of fertility) reports a possible increase in recent years, from 106 deaths per 1000 infants earlier this decade to 111 deaths in 1987.

These factors suggest that Tanzania will have to undertake a more comprehensive and substantial family planning program in order to realize the economic progress it seeks.

THAILAND

1990 Population: 56.5 m.
2000 Population: 66 m.
Doubling Time: 41 Years

Thailand has enjoyed substantial success with its population program. The government's program to promote family planning was launched in 1970 and has been administered consistently and vigorously since. In the 10 years following that introduction, population growth fell from a steep 3.2 percent to 1.9 percent.

Knowledge of family planning methods is now nearly universal in Thailand, and contraceptive use is approaching levels found in many developed countries. In 1981, 59 percent of married Thai women were using birth control, and that figure is now estimated to be between 65 and 70 percent.

Thailand has been so successful, first, because the government had a strong family planning base with which to work. Scattered family planning efforts had begun privately in the early 1960s and by the time the government initiated its program in 1970, some 53 percent of women surveyed knew of at least one method of birth control. Thus, the government had something of a headstart when it undertook its efforts.

But once the government did become involved, its program quickly surpassed private efforts. The government's program of establishing widely dispersed family planning outlets made birth control almost universally available, so that by the early 1980s, three-quarters of users said they received their family planning services through government outlets (rather than private clinics or doctors).

A good deal of the credit must be given to one man, Mechai Viravaidya, the founder and longtime director of Thailand's Population and Community Development Association. Mechai spearheaded Thailand's innovative efforts to increase the availability of contraceptives. Through a package of marketing incentives, condoms are often readily available in Thailand from street vendors, taxi drivers, and distributors at sporting events and religious festivals.

UNITED NATIONS

Taking a bath amid slums

Even Thailand, however, will double its population in just 41 years at current growth rates. While that figure represents a laudable improvement over several decades ago, it can be considered a "success" only on a relative scale, when compared to the truly grim situation faced by so many other countries in the developing world.

Thai fertility now averages 3.5 children per woman. The country's government remains committed to achieving replacement fertility by the year 2000 and that seems a realistic goal given the program's record of progress.

TURKEY

1990 Population: 56.6 m.
2000 Population: 69 m.
Doubling Time: 32 Years

The Turkish government abandoned its long-standing pronatalist population policy in the early 1960s, but then considered the reduction of population growth to be an indirect objective to be achieved through general economic development. Only in the past decade has the government begun to promote family planning as an independent means of curbing population expansion.

In the 1980s, the government undertook several changes to improve its population policy. Article 41 of the 1982 Constitution makes it a government obligation to protect family welfare and extend family planning services to the people. Legislation was enacted in 1983 to expand significantly the methods of family planning available to couples. Compulsory two-year rural service was also required of new medical graduates. And, finally, the government restructured its program to encourage the distribution of family planning services through rural midwives.

These efforts have helped to improve rural health conditions and curb fertility, which although still high is now down to an average of 4 children per woman.

FAO

Vietnam's population is growing more swiftly

VIETNAM

1990 Population: 68.5 m.
2000 Population: 87 m.
Doubling Time: 27 Years

Although the Vietnamese government recognizes the importance of curbing population growth and has undertaken efforts to extend family planning services, the government's program appears to have failed to meet its population goals.

In the early 1980s, the government set a goal of decreasing the rate of population growth from its 1981 level of 2.2 percent to 1.7 percent by 1985. Population was growing in 1987, however, by 2.6 percent, a significant increase from 1981 levels.

The government appears to have had greater success with its goals for reducing infant mortality. Infant mortality stood at the beginning of this decade at 76 deaths per 1000 infants, according to U.N. figures; by 1987, that figure may have fallen to as few as 55 deaths. This reduction could lead eventually to reduced fertility as couples realize their offspring have a greater chance for survival. But the government clearly must improve its delivery of family planning services if growth is to decline significantly.

ZAIRE

1990 Population: 36.0 m.
2000 Population: 50 m.
Doubling Time: 23 Years

Zaire is on the leading edge of a continent-wide change in thinking about population growth. Until relatively recently, the government of Zaire, like most of its neighbors, was generally satisfied with its rapid population growth and did not view the 3-percent population growth rate as a threat to the country's economic development hopes. During the mid-1980s, however, Zaire has taken a giant forward leap and has come to recognize that population growth must be tamed if the nation is to break out of the cycle of economic stagnation.

Thanks largely to the counsel of U.N. and U.S. aid officials, officers at all levels of Zaire's government have realized the damaging effects of population expansion. As a result of this spreading awareness, Zaire established a Commission on Population and Development and in December of 1986 drafted a national policy on population. That policy draft has won prelminary government approval and is expected to be adopted shortly by President Mobutu Sese Seko.

FAO

Zaire:
A new policy
holds promise
□□□□□

Zaire is now moving forward with plans to extend awareness of the implications of overpopulation to all of its citizens. Given sustained international support, Zaire is expected to have a major population program in place by the end of this decade. Its recent commitment is truly a dramatic development and provides a positive example for other African nations, such as Benin, Togo, and Botswana, which are now beginning to draft similar national policies.

GLOBAL SUMMARY

1990 Population: 5.33 b.
2000 Population: 6.4 b.
Doubling Time: 39 Years

EAST ASIA: East Asia boasts some of the developing world's greatest success stories with regard to curbing population growth. Thailand, Indonesia, South Korea, and Taiwan all have securely-established family planning programs and important gains to show for them. In addition, China's population program has made significant inroads toward reduction in the fertility of the entire region.

Yet those successes must be contrasted against other nations in the region. The governments of Burma and Malaysia maintain pronatalist policies. And programs in Vietnam and the Philippines will require greater commitments to achieve more substantial gains.

MIDDLE AND NEAR EAST: The nations of the Indian subcontinent—Pakistan, India, Nepal, Sri Lanka, and Bangladesh—have all recognized the necessity of curbing population growth for eventual economic development. Family planning programs in these nations were among the first to be established in the developing world and financial commitments to them remain high.

UNITED NATIONS

Middle and Near East: unprecedented growth
□ □ □ □ □

Gains from these efforts, however, have been slower in coming than to many of their eastern neighbors. While knowledge and acceptance of family planning among the populations is very good, limited availability of services and contraceptives has undercut greater progress. With very large populations and high growth rates, the Indian subcontinent's future progress is vital to global reductions.

Population growth rates are even higher in many of the nations to the west of Pakistan. Iran, Iraq, Jordan, Syria, Saudi Arabia, Oman, North and South Yemen, and Kuwait are all growing at 3 percent or faster. Even this rate is likely to increase in some countries; in Jordan, for example, 55 percent of the population is under the age of 15 and will soon enter its reproductive years.

The smaller base populations of these countries, however, make their growth rates somewhat less alarming.

AFRICA: Africa is the world's fastest growing continent. At its present growth rate of 3 percent, Africa's 646 million population will double in just 20 years and triple by 2025. The continent includes the world's fastest growing nation, Kenya, and the world's poorest, Ethiopia.

Several African nations have undertaken promising programs to help their people prevent unwanted pregnancies. The commitment currently evidenced by the governments of Kenya, Nigeria, Zambia, Botswana, Zaire and Zimbabwe is encouraging. But with continent-wide fertility still averaging more than six children per woman, significant reductions in African population expansion will be as expensive and hard-won as they will be vitally important to world stability and to the improvement of the quality of life for its people.

LATIN AMERICA: Several Latin American countries, including Mexico, Colombia, Peru, and Brazil, have well-established and productive family planning efforts. In addition, Argentina, Chile, and Uruguay have reduced their growth rates to an admirable 1.6 percent or below.

Their successes, however, have been diluted by unabated rapid population growth in parts of Central America and the Caribbean. The populations of Honduras, Guatemala, and Nicaragua, for example, are all growing at faster than 3 percent per year. Furthermore, Mexico's gains through its innovative social-marketing program are jeopardized by the weakening of its oil-based economy.

FAO

In Latin America, progress has been uneven

THE INDUSTRIALIZED "WEST": The industrialized nations of North America, Western Europe, and the Pacific (Australia, New Zealand, and Japan) are characterized by slow or negligible population growth and high standards of living. After the West's post-war "baby boom" subsided around 1965, fertility rates began to fall in each country and they are still edging downward.

Population growth is slowest in Western Europe. The populations of Denmark, Austria, and West Germany are actually not growing at all. France, with population growing at a slight 0.4 percent annually, has adopted a policy to encourage French couples to have more children.

The populations of the other industrialized Western nations—the United States, Canada, Japan, Australia, and New Zealand—are each growing somewhat more than their European counterparts, but still no more than 0.8 percent per year. At such rates, it would take these countries roughly 100 years to double their populations.

In all of the industrialized Western nations, the absence of rapid population growth has permitted greater investment in economic and social development.

THE INDUSTRIALIZED "EAST": Population growth rates in the Soviet Union and Eastern Europe are generally comparable to those in the industrialized West. Just as in the West, birth rates in the East bloc nations fell following a post-World War II "baby boom."

Unlike most Western nations, however, the nations of the East bloc have adopted pro-natalist policies designed to reverse the slowing-down of their population growth. These policies include economic incentives such as birth grants, paid maternity leave, childcare allowances, and subsidies for nurseries, school meals, transportation, and housing. In addition, many of these nations have enacted laws forbidding or restricting abortion. The only exception to this broad pro-natalist trend is Yugoslavia, which maintains a constitutional guarantee of the right to family planning.

Despite such incentives, however, many of which date back 20 years, there has been no meaningful increase in fertility. In fact, abortion rates remain very high in some Eastern-bloc nations, according to the Transnational Family Research Institute. New statistics from the Soviet Union obtained as a result of the new Russian "glasnost," or openness policy, report that two out of every three pregnancies there end in abortion, many of which are illegal. Furthermore, fully 75 percent of Soviet women have had at least one abortion, many of them having upwards of five abortions (such figures are much higher than in the United States, where 30 percent of pregnancies result in abortions). The continuing high incidence of abortion in the Soviet Union underscores the degree to which pro-natalist policies there have failed and suggests that fertility will remain relatively low.

UNITED NATIONS

In Brazil, birth rates are coming down

Summary

The experiences of the 20 developing nations highlighted in the preceding section suggest that over the past two decades many have heeded the message traditionally pressed by the United States and other industrialized nations that controlling population growth is an essential prerequisite to economic development. Some who learned that lesson early, like the nations of East Asia, have made substantial progress. Some others, like Mexico and Brazil, reached that conclusion somewhat later but have begun making up for lost time.

Still others, like many of the African nations, have only very recently demonstrated a willingness to tackle the problem, if necessary foreign assistance can be found. Finally, there remain a dwindling handful of Third World nations that cling to the belief that population pressures will be solved naturally through economic development. These nations, which include some of the developing world's poorest (such as Burma, Mongolia, Mauritania, and Mozambique), consider independent efforts to curb fertility to be unnecessary or even undesirable.

All of the family planning programs in operation throughout the developing world, however, even the long-established and successful, will require steadily increasing financial commitments and sustained political support in the coming years in order to reach steadily growing numbers of reproductive-age couples. If either financial support or political will slackens, many of the hard-fought gains in parts of Asia, Africa, and Latin America will be seriously eroded or erased.

There have been a few observers who have mistakenly assumed that because population growth rates have declined in all of the industrialized world and much of the developing world, there is no longer a "crisis" in world population. This is a dangerously misguided conclusion.

It is true that the world's "developed" nations have generally achieved very low population growth, but these nations account for only 25 percent of the world's population. It is also true that many developing nations have slowed their rates of population growth, but even the most successful among them are still growing quickly.

UNITED NATIONS

China: the one-child family is taking hold
□ □ □ □ □

Any temptation toward complacency should be dispelled by noting that barely 20 percent of Third World couples now use family planning. If the world is to reach replacement fertility by 2000, that use must increase very soon to 80 percent, a level not often seen even in developed Western societies.

Clearly, the "population explosion" is still very much in evidence. And, while the world has made commendable headway over the past 20 years, much more remains to be done.

The industrialized nations of North America and Western Europe spent much of the 1960s and 1970s engaged in a determined and sometimes arduous effort to persuade the governments of the developing world that they should act to control their population growth. Although some developing nations, including Colombia, Zimbabwe, and South Korea, required no persuasion, the majority of the Third World still viewed their booming populations as a stimulant, and not a hindrance, to their economic development. Some in the Third World, where national strength is sometimes seen as tied to population size, were initially suspicious about outside efforts to influence their fertility. Slowly, however—thanks in part to unwavering counsel from the United States and other industrialized countries, and in part to the increasingly unmistakable damage caused by unchecked growth—most Third World countries now seek slower growth.

RECENT SETBACKS IN U.S. ASSISTANCE

The investment made by the United States and its allies in international development is long-term. Wisely, it is not aimed at overnight solutions, and its eventual success depends upon sustained and even support.

This policy of counsel and assistance has already yielded tangible gains. Lowered fertility and growth rates virtually the world over are due in no small part to external assistance. The happy progress seen in Thailand, Tunisia, Colombia, and elsewhere is the early fruit of this investment. Furthermore, across Africa, where high fertility has been the least receptive to change, there is now an emerging commitment to action on the population issue—a commitment which can be credited in good part to an intelligent and consistent donor country partnership. By all evidence, the international donor community is on the verge of reaping the returns on its investment in this continent so crucial to world progress.

That international partnership, and the progress it is beginning to produce, is now threatened, however, by faltering U.S. policy. After two decades of telling the developing world that it is not sufficient to wait for economic progress to "solve" the problem of rapid population growth, the U.S. government abruptly reversed this position at the 1984 United Nations Conference on World Population in Mexico City. America spent 20 years preaching independent efforts to moderate rapid population growth as a necessary component of any economic development plan. And just as the developing world was beginning to agree, the United States changed its mind. This view left the United States virtually alone among the 148 countries represented at the conference.

Whereas the other conference delegates agreed with the traditional U.S. view that real economic progress is not possible in the Third World in the presence of unchecked explosive population growth, the new U.S. delegates adopted the view that population growth was a "neutral" factor in economic development.

There are other manifestations as well of declining U.S. leadership in the struggle for population stabilization, particularly leadership among other industrialized donor nations. In 1980, the U.S. National Security Council warned, "By virtue of experience and resources, the U.S. cannot relinquish the leadership in this area. . . . The United States should seek to keep the population problem at the forefront of the world's agendas, as a matter of urgent global priority . . . (and) the U.S. should consult with other donor governments at highest policy levels, e.g., the Economic Summit meetings." For several years, that advice was followed, and the United States ensured that population growth was discussed when the leaders of the world's seven most powerful industrialized democracies met at their annual summits. In the official conference declaration following the 1981 economic summit in Ottawa, Canada, for instance, the leaders of the United States, Canada, Japan, Great Britain, France, West Germany, and Italy agreed:

UNITED NATIONS

A woman bagging rice in Liberia

> "We are deeply concerned about the implications of world population growth. Many developing countries are taking action to deal with that problem, in ways sensitive to human values and dignity. . . . We recognize the importance of these issues and will place greater emphasis on international efforts in these areas."

Such agreements among seven of the world's most influential donor nations were important and held real potential to advance international efforts to establish and realize population goals.

Since 1982, however, expressions of concern over rapid world population growth have been dropped from the summits and the word "population" has been conspicuously absent from subsequent confer-

Recent Setbacks in U.S. Assistance

ence declarations. As a result, the summit statements speak of the need for providing employment opportunities for the young, and now ignore the fact that rapid population growth will require the Third World to create 800 million new jobs in the next 13 years. The declarations decry pollution and the loss of resources vital to the world economy, while neglecting the pivotal role that population growth plays in accelerating that loss. And, finally, the summit delegates since 1982 have lamented the persistent difficulty for Third World nations in handling the burden of international debt, while setting aside the fact that overpopulation cripples developing economies and smothers the economic aspirations of the Third World. Beginning in 1983, when the United States played host to the summit in Williamsburg, Virginia, the delegates have surveyed the world economy with one blind eye, taking in the negative consequences of overpopulation without seeing the cause.

This sudden impairment must be attributed to the Reagan Administration's new view that rapid population growth is irrelevant to economic development plans in the developing world and to the Administration's influence with the other summit delegates.

This conclusion is reinforced by recent correspondence with European governments in which U.S. allies have underscored their unwavering commitment to population assistance. In a letter to the Population Institute following the 1987 Venice summit, an official of the British Overseas Development Administration, writing on behalf of Prime Minister Margaret Thatcher, emphasized that Britain is moving forward with population assistance despite any weaknesses in U.S. resolve:

WHITE HOUSE

1987 Venice Summit: population was not on the agenda

"The [summit] meeting discussed a wide range of economic subjects, including the problems of developing countries. In particular, attention was focused on the British Chancellor of the Exchequer's recent initiative on the need for special consideration for the poorest indebted countries in Africa. Although population growth is not specifically mentioned in the [summit] Declaration, I am sure that, in looking at the problems of the poorest countries, the meeting was mindful of the relationship between high population growth rates and economic and social development. . . . The British Government has always acknowledged the importance of population programmes in the development process and given them a high priority in its overseas aid programme."

The West German government, also in 1987 correspondence, has similarly underscored its commitment: "The Federal German Government declares its readiness to promote population activities in developing countries to an even greater extent in the future." It should also be noted that other summit participants, including Japan and Canada, have recently increased their financial contributions to the United Nations Fund for Population Activities. All this has essentially left the United States alone among its industrialized Western allies in pulling back from the effort to win the fight against rapid population growth.

What damage this confusing reversal of U.S. policy has caused to the American (and international) objective of a more stable world population has been seriously compounded by steadily declining U.S. financial commitments to international population assistance.

WHITE HOUSE

President Reagan gets tough
□ □ □ □ □

U.S. Withdrawal from International Efforts

Traditionally, the channel through which the United States made its most significant contribution to world population stabilization was not direct, bilateral aid, but U.S. financial support for two international family planning programs, as well as a host of non-governmental organizations. The two major programs—the United Nations Fund for Population Activities (UNFPA) and the International Planned Parenthood Federation (IPPF)—as well as their non-governmental colleagues, had several distinct advantages over direct "government-to-government" aid.

For one thing, the U.S. government is reluctant to enter, or is not always welcome in some Third World countries with sensitive political situations. Using multi-lateral, umbrella organizations such as UNFPA and IPPF provides the United States with a vehicle for accomplishing its population policy objectives without upsetting delicate relationships with these foreign governments. A second advantage is that U.S. contributions to international agencies can encourage other donor nations to increase their contributions as well, thereby having a "multiplier effect" for its policy objectives.

The 1980 policy paper drafted by the National Security Council Ad Hoc Group on Population Policy explained this approach:

> "The U.S. has recognized that, for many reasons, bilateral population programs may not always be the most appropriate way to assist many developing countries: this is reflected in the fact

that over half of AID's budget currently [in 1980] goes to private intermediary agencies (34 percent) and UNFPA (16 percent).

The private organizations generally enjoy substantial public support in countries where they operate, and have pioneered innovative approaches more easily than official programs. The largest of these agencies, IPPF, with affiliates in nearly 100 countries, also attracts funds from other donor governments, and particularly merits expanded U.S. support. . . . We believe that U.S. support to UNFPA, consistent with the NSC recommendation of 1975, should be significantly expanded beyond current levels."

This was the recommendation of a federal policy group made up of officials from the National Security Council and 17 other U.S. government departments and agencies—a group serving under both Democratic and Republican administrations. It was based not on domestic political considerations, but upon a sound and rational assessment of U.S. security interests.

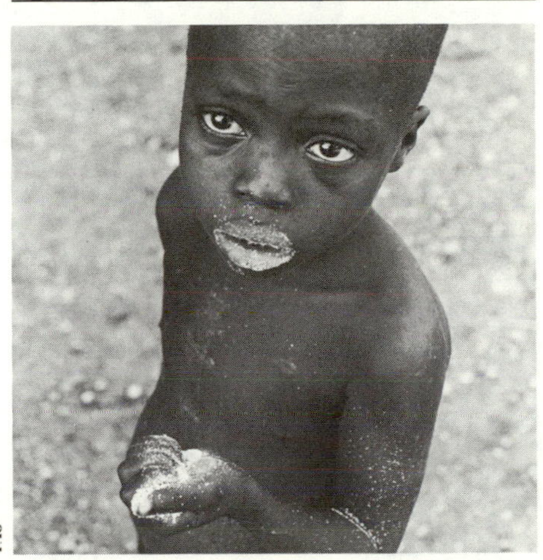
FAO

African children grow weak

In the past three years, however, in a sharp departure from traditional, bipartisan U.S. population policy, the U.S. government has withdrawn its support from both IPPF and UNFPA, casting serious doubts on the futures of these and other cooperative international efforts.

The reason given by the United States for cutting off its support in both cases was the same—opposition to abortion. And yet in both cases, the withdrawal of support has not caused a decline in abortions and may well have caused an increase.

The first to lose U.S. aid was IPPF, the global arm of the respected American family planning organization. The program was a casualty of the new U.S. population policy unveiled at the Mexico City conference. Part of that policy forbids U.S. financial support to any private organization that counsels, refers, or provides abortion services to women, even if those services are paid for entirely by private contributions.

It should be noted that an amendment to the Foreign Assistance Act, offered by Senator Jesse Helms and passed by Congress in 1973, already prohibited any U.S. tax dollars from being used to "pay for the performance of abortions as a method of family planning or to motivate or coerce any person to practice abortions." The new "Mexico City Policy" essentially extended that prohibition to cover not only tax dollars, but even private dollars spent by a tax-supported institution. As with the 1973 law, the new policy prohibited support for abortions of any kind, including the strictly voluntary abortions provided by IPPF and other family planning organizations.

In IPPF's case, U.S. government aid, in accordance with the 1973 law, did not go toward abortion-related services. Furthermore, of IPPF's private, non-restricted budget, less than one half of one percent actually went toward providing voluntary abortions. Nonetheless, the new U.S. regulation was pressed by some activists as grounds for cutting off U.S. support for IPPF, which remains by far the most effective and accomplished private family planning organization active in the Third World.

Efforts to correct this policy are already underway in Congress. The U.S. Senate Committee on Foreign Relations, in its 1988 authorizing legislation, has sought to bring administration policy back into line with the laws established by Congress. The Committee has adopted an amendment offered by Kansas Republican Senator Nancy Kassebaum that would prevent the administration from penalizing multilateral or non-governmental organizations from carrying out lawful activities with private funds. In its report on the amendment, the Committee stressed that its action is specifically intended to overturn the administration's policy and added, "The so-called Mexico City policy announced by the administration in 1984 simply went beyond any requirement of law."

UNITED NATIONS

A Chinese woman carries her grandchild
□□□□□

The second international organization to lose U.S. aid was the UNFPA. The UNFPA is the largest multi-lateral, international organization working to promote family planning and population stabilization in the developing world and it derives most of its annual budget from support from industrialized Western member states.

U.S. aid to UNFPA was reduced by $10 million in fiscal year 1985 and was eliminated entirely in 1986 and 1987. The impact on UNFPA's budget is substantial because the United States had originally pledged to contribute $46 million in 1985. That pledge had already been incorporated into UNFPA's extended budget for program planning. Thus, the elimination of all U.S. aid meant a long-range disruption to UNFPA's efforts. The U.S. actions to cut off aid were taken to protest what the administration believes is a coercive abortion policy in China.

In choking off funds to UNFPA in August 1986, the administration cited a provision in the 1985 Foreign Assistance Act that prohibits U.S. aid to any organization which "participates in the management" of a program of coerced abortions and involuntary sterilizations. The administration argued that because UNFPA contributions make up one percent of China's population program budget, the United States cannot legally support UNFPA.

A number of members of Congress from both political parties have disputed the administration's interpretation. They have pointed out that U.S. contributions to the UNFPA program were segregated into a separate account to ensure that no U.S. funds went to China (the account's integrity was confirmed in subsequent audits by representatives of the Secretary of State, the Agency for International Development, and the U.S. Permanent Representative to the United Nations), and that, at any rate, such a contribution could not be construed as "participation in the management" of China's $1-billion program.

UNITED NATIONS

Shrinking aid, spreading poverty

One such critic is Senator Daniel Inouye, a Democrat from Hawaii. As chairman of the Senate Appropriations Subcommittee on Foreign Operations and as the Senate sponsor of the disputed provision, Senator Inouye wrote to Secretary of State George P. Shultz in July of 1987 requesting that Secretary Shultz "personally review" the administration's decision regarding UNFPA. Senator Inouye provides a valuable look inside the intent of Congress in writing this contentious provision and his letter is worth citing at length:

"As one of the authors of the amendment in question, it is my contention that, in order to rightfully invoke this amendment as the reason for withdrawal of U.S. support from UNFPA, it must be determined that 1) the People's Republic of China does, in fact, have a program of coercive abortion and 2) that the UNFPA supports or participates in the management of such a program. I made these points repeatedly in discussion of my amendment before the Senate Committee on Appropriations and also in debate on the Senate floor. The legislative history of this interpretation is clear.

"The judgement must be whether the UNFPA programs in China have worked to mitigate the incidence of abortion in China and whether continued U.S. participation in the premier international family planning organization serves American ideals and interests. As you study this matter to reach an informed judgement, I hope you will consider the following factors.

"First, with respect to the question of coercive abortion in the UNFPA programs in China, [U.S. AID Director M. Peter] McPherson has informed me that he believes that 'UNFPA does not include coercive abortion or involuntary sterilization in its own programs in China.' This confirms an Agency for International Development internal review conducted in April of 1985 which found no coercive abortion in the UNFPA program.

"On the second point, that of the actual existence of a program of coercive abortion in China, I would note that in response to a question I posed to you during Senate hearings on the fiscal year 1986 Foreign Assistance Appropriations request, you indicated that such a program does not exist. The question I asked was, 'If it is found that the People's Republic of China sanctions coerced abortion . . . will the Administration withhold 'military technology cooperation?' Your reply was, I believe, a correct and accurate statement. You said, 'It is our understanding that the Chinese Government does not sanction forced abortion, and has made clear the central government's stand against the practice, as reflected in statements by leading officials.'

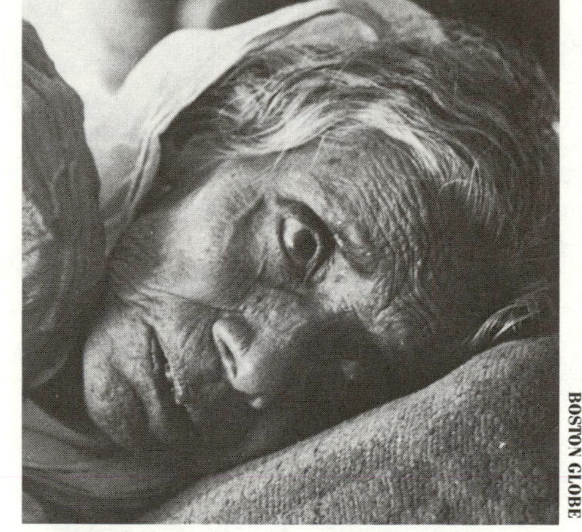
BOSTON GLOBE

The suffering of the old can be intensified by the pressures of overpopulation

"Mr. Secretary, I do not know of any documented evidence of a program of coerced abortion in the People's Republic of China. In April of this year, I sent a Staff Delegation to China to review the Chinese program and UNFPA activities. A thorough review of UNFPA activities in China led the Staff Delegation to the firm conclusion that there is no evidence whatsoever that the UNFPA supports or participates in a program of coerced abortion in China. I hope that your review of this matter will lead to the same conclusion."

Not satisfied to wait for a re-interpretation by the administration of the Kemp-Inouye Amendment, some members of Congress are working to rewrite the provision to make it less pliable to misinterpretation. Congressional efforts similar to those seeking to overturn the Mexico City Policy are pending to restore U.S. funding of UNFPA. Republican Senator Daniel Evans of Washington has offered an amendment to the Foreign Assistance Act that aims to eliminate any ambiguity in the law governing U.S. aid. The Evans Amendment, which has been approved by the Senate Foreign Relations Committee, would prohibit U.S. assistance to any organization "which directly participates in coercive abortion or involuntary sterilization." In its official legislative report, the Committee made its position clear on the issue: "The decision to withhold U.S. funds from UNFPA is unconscionable and unjustified. The Committee, in adopting this provision, intends that by clarifying Congressional intent the U.S. contribution to UNFPA will be resumed in fiscal year 1988."

Recent Setbacks in U.S. Assistance
□

Declining U.S. Aid

It should be noted that population assistance programs have never constituted a large part of the U.S. foreign aid budget. Programs to promote family planning and stable population growth around the world make up only 4 percent of U.S. humanitarian assistance. The portion allocated for population programs is further restricted because foreign aid dollars go first to the State Department's priority clients: Israel, Egypt, Pakistan, and, more recently, Ireland. Only after priority programs in those nations have been funded, and after money is set aside for programs to curb terrorism and narcotics traffic, are the remaining programs—including all other foreign development aid and, finally, population assistance—permitted to compete for the funds left over.

UNITED NATIONS

Digging for water in Mozambique
□ □ □ □ □

In recent years, those leftover funds have dwindled. The U.S. government's commitment to international population assistance (which is part of the budget of the U.S. Agency for International Development) has dropped from $290 million in FY84 to $250 million in FY85, to $235 million in FY86. The FY87 allocation of $236.5 million was later reduced by 15 percent to create an emergency relief set-aside fund. For FY88, the Reagan administration has sought to erode the population assistance budget further, to $207 million, although the House Foreign Affairs Committee has moved to increase that to $222 million (still nearly $15 million less than was budgeted in the last fiscal year).

The sudden reversal of long-standing U.S. policy encouraging wise population strategies and the controversial withdrawal of U.S. support from UNFPA and IPPF have deeply concerned our Western allies and our friends in the Third World. They cannot understand an American policy whose stated purpose is in opposition to abortion and yet whose effect will be precisely to cause more unwanted pregnancies and, thus, more abortions.

They do not understand why the United States, which for so long was leading forward-looking nations in the search for solutions, has now decided, in effect, to sit on its hands with regard to world population.

To many nations in the developing world, for whom mounting population pressures are not abstract policy issues but are a matter of life and death, the U.S. retreat from international cooperative efforts seems capricious and even mean-spirited.

This perception of the United States is too costly in the strategically important Third World. The stakes are too high, and the immediate opportunities for political, social, and economic progress are too great to shrug off.

UNITED NATIONS

Children weave mats in Bangladesh

DANGEROUS MYTHS, STARK REALITIES

Anyone who struggles to understand the complexities of population and its relationship with economics, societies, and the environment runs into a handful of common and persistent misconceptions about population dynamics. It is perhaps understandable that such misconceptions arise, for two reasons in particular.

First, demography is an imprecise science. By its very nature, it deals in projections and estimations. It is, therefore, vulnerable to those who would misinterpret or, in some cases, deliberately distort the facts that are known. Second, the provision of population assistance and family planning services touches on very sensitive and personal issues; it involves the most intimate of human relations and goes to the heart of human rights: the decision about whether and when to have children.

All of the misconceptions that arise, however, impede the delivery of services and serve as obstacles that must be overcome in the effort to achieve world population stabilization. It is valuable to address some of the most common myths.

1. Myth: The "Population Explosion" is Over.

Some observers have noted that birth rates are falling in most of the world's nations and concluded that, therefore, the world has conquered its population problem. This misconception is fueled further by the fact that the nations of the industrialized world (where most of these observers reside) have brought their fertility down to replacement levels or below.

The fact of the matter is, however, that while many countries have made admirable and encouraging progress, the world's overall population continues to grow at an astonishing rate—last year alone, it grew by 93 million people. This is because fertility in many developing countries was so high to begin with. Even countries that have substantially reduced fertility, such as Thailand, Indonesia, and Colombia, are successful only in comparison to the grim situations in many other Third World countries. The populations of those three "success stories" will still double in just 33 years at present growth rates. And there are many other developing nations in which progress has been slower in coming or that maintain pro-natalist policies.

All in all, with the world doubling its population in barely 40 years at current rates, and with 3 billion young people entering their reproductive years over the next generation, the task of curbing rapid population growth remains as challenging as ever. Progress toward the goal should not be mistaken for final victory.

2. Myth: Population Growth is Irrelevant to Economic Development.

This is the misconception now embodied in current U.S. policy. It holds that money spent on family planning and population programs in Third World countries is essentially a distraction or a diversion of money that could have been spent on economic development projects. It holds that investments in family planning do not contribute to the well-being of the developing society.

The fallacy of this argument becomes apparent when one considers the actual experiences of developing nations. Tracking the per capita economic expansion of countries with and without rapid population growth is an illuminating exercise. In countries with relatively stable populations, each expansion of the Gross National Product is shared by the citizenry and per capita income—each person's economic well-being—rises. In countries with rapidly expanding populations, each additional increment in the Gross National Product must go toward supporting each additional individual; the number of new persons almost always grows faster than the number of new dollars in the Gross National Product, and per capita income remains stagnant or declines.

UNITED NATIONS

In the developing world, the young feel the impact of population growth

As an example, consider the recent experiences of Japan and Brazil. Both countries have enjoyed vigorous economic growth over the past quarter-century with their Gross National Products expanding by 5 to 10 percent annually. Furthermore, both countries started the 25-year period with roughly similar per capita GNPs ($900 per person in Brazil and $1,400 per person in Japan in 1960). But the similarities end there. In the years that followed, Brazil's population grew rapidly, while Japan's was much more stable. Consequently, Brazil's economic growth was diluted among ever growing numbers of people, while Japan's translated into real improvements in the quality of life for the population. Today, Japan's per capita GNP is $16,000; Brazil's is $2,000.

No less a fiscal conservative than Jeanne Kirkpatrick, President Reagan's first Ambassador to the United Nations, has said that providing economic aid to the Third World without working also to curb rapid population growth is like "pouring water into a bucket with a hole in it."

Ambassador Kirkpatrick has been joined by other Reagan Administration foreign policy experts in recognizing this fundamental relationship. Secretary of State George P. Shultz testified before the House Committee on Foreign Affairs that "rampant population growth underlies the Third World's poverty and poses a major long-term threat to political stability and our planet's resource base." Deputy Secretary of State John Whitehead carried that point further in a 1987 speech on the challenge of African development for U.S. policy: "The current rate of population growth of around 3 percent a year threatens Africa with disaster. Should a burgeoning population outstrip economic growth, living standards will decline and the African environment will be further degraded as more and more people try to eke out a living from marginal land."

It is most unfortunate that the Administration has disregarded the common-sense truth spoken by its own specialists in foreign policy. Instead of taking the advice of its experts on international development, the Administration has listened to ideologues opposed to family planning and adopted the myth that rapid population growth has no economic impact.

WORLD BANK

African agricultural production cannot keep up with population growth
□□□□□

3. *Myth: "Free Enterprise is the Best Contraceptive."*

There is another myth associated with the "Mexico City Policy." It starts out reasonably with the premise that free enterprise contributes to rising standards of living, which, in turn, help to stabilize population growth. But it finishes with the flawed conclusion that, therefore, independent efforts to reduce fertility are not really necessary.

The Americans who preach this view to the developing world base their conclusions on the observation that rapid population growth has disappeared from the world's leading free-market nations, including the United States, Canada, Japan, and the countries of Western Europe. They point out that population growth subsided in these nations with the emergence of industrialization and strong economic growth. What the Third World needs, they say, is not population assistance, but capitalism and robust economic growth made possible by free enterprise.

"Follow our example and adopt the free market," is these Americans' pat response to developing nations that appeal for help with their problems of booming population growth, crippling foreign debt, struggling economies, and spreading poverty. This advice translates into the slogan, "Capitalism is the best contraceptive"—the free market will cure economic woes and, once poverty has been solved, couples will naturally desire fewer children.

There can be no doubt that significant economic growth contributes to population stabilization. But, the Third World's economic problems are clearly too deep and complex to be solved overnight; meanwhile, the world, already pressed with 5 billion will be adding another billion people every 11 years.

The problem with the "free market" myth is three-fold. First, it ignores the more than 400 million people in the developing world who *already* desire smaller families but lack access to the education and means to avoid future pregnancies.

UNITED NATIONS

Much labor in Bangladesh must be done by hand
□ □ □ □ □

Second, it draws a false comparison between the situations faced by pre-industrial Europe and modern-day developing countries. One reason that Europe was able to handle the rapid population growth it experienced 200 years ago was that its growing population had plenty of room to expand. Europe was able to navigate the "demographic transition" from pre-industrial rapid population growth to post-industrial stable populations while exporting many hundreds of thousands of people overseas to settle North America, Australia, South Africa, and other areas then sparsely settled. Europe also started with a relatively small population and had the breathing room of 150 years over which to accomplish this economic and social transformation.

The nations of present-day Africa, Asia, and Latin America do not have such comfortable circumstances. There are few open spaces left on the earth to be settled by booming populations. Furthermore, the developing nations of the Third World are starting with much larger populations and with much more severe and immediate population pressures. With their populations already pressing environmental "carrying capacities" and yet still doubling every 20 years, these nations do not have the economic and social options that made Europe's industrialization so successful. What worked for 18th Century Europe is simply not a suitable prescription for late 20th Century Africa and Latin America.

The third and perhaps the most serious error underlying this myth is that it denies the clear fact that fertility rates ignore the imaginary boundaries established by economic theorists. The populations of Tanzania and Nicaragua, for example, two countries with centrally-planned economies, are growing by more than 3 percent each year, but so are the populations of free-market Liberia and Guatemala. Furthermore, some of the most dramatic declines in fertility have occurred in nations lacking the benefit of the free market. Cuba and China are prime examples. Moreover, the Soviet Union and its Eastern European allies have population growth rates similar to those found in the United States and its Western European allies.

All of these case histories contradict the suggestion that the presence of free market economies alone is sufficient to tame rapid population growth. All of these case examples do, however, support the far more reasonable observation that fertility rates are a function of both economic well-being and knowledge and access to family planning services. In countries where family planning is readily available and where smaller family size is desired, fertility declines—regardless of the economy's philosophical orientation.

UNITED NATIONS

China's declining fertility has contributed to rising living standards
□ □ □ □ □

This fact does not dispute the virtues of the free market system. A number of developing countries might well benefit from adoption of capitalist economies. But an affection for the free market should not delude American observers to believe, as it apparently has some, that free enterprise is a substitution for the ability of couples to determine freely the number and spacing of their children.

This particular myth can be damaging when it leads Americans to believe that they can "solve" the population crisis by offering high-sounding sermons on capitalism in place of doing the hard work of extending economic assistance and the availability of family planning.

4. Myth: The "Real" Population Problem is Western "Depopulation".

One of the most recent obstacles encountered in the road to population stabilization has been the view that the United States and other industrialized Western nations are not breeding fast enough. The proponents of this view look at the disparity between stable industrialized populations and booming Third World expansion and conclude that the problem is not one of Third World overpopulation, but Western "underpopulation." They also point with alarm to pro-natalist policies in the Soviet Union and most East bloc countries. Finally, these observers cite declining fertility rates in North America, Japan, and Western Europe and fear that "Western culture" will decline along with birth rates.

This argument has several serious flaws. First, there is no reason to predict that fertility in Western industrialized nations will continue to decline and that population there will actually begin to decrease. There have always been cycles of surges and recessions in fertility and historical evidence suggests strongly that, on balance, these populations will stabilize or continue to grow in slight increments. Consider that during a downward cycle in 1931, demographers predicted that England's population would drop below 10 million early in the 21st Century. After a post-World War II "baby boom," however, its population was projected to reach 75 million by the year 2000. As it actually turned out, however, the United Kingdom's current population is approximately 57 million and is now projected to be 58.2 million in the year 2100.

UNICEF

Thai children at supper. Thai women are desiring smaller families □□□□□

Second, even if Western populations did shrink somewhat, the size of a country's population does not determine its economic or military strength. Were this true, China, with a population four times that of the United States, would be by far the most powerful nation on earth. But both China and India, the world's second most populous nation, are stuggling to assemble economic and military power. A far more important determinant of a nation's power and well-being is its ability to balance population with resources and to employ technology and economic resources to maximum advantage. This explains why nations with relatively stable populations—like West Germany, the United States, and Japan—exercise impressive and growing economic power and why large nations with burgeoning populations do not.

Third, there is no reason to predict that the industrialized nations of the communist bloc will actually increase their populations through pro-natalist policies. The system of incentives to encourage births has been on the books in these nations for 20 years and it has proved an utter failure. Fertility in these countries remains low and comparable to that in Western industrialized nations. Annual population growth in the Soviet Union is 1.0 percent, compared to 0.7 percent in the

United States; in Western Europe, annual growth is 0.2 percent, compared to 0.3 percent in Eastern Europe.

The persistence of the similarity in these figures suggests that the communist pro-natalist policies are not working and that larger economic forces in both Western and Eastern societies are more important in determining fertility. At bottom, few couples can be persuaded with passing government incentives to have more children than they actually want.

It is absolutely true that the world is largely divided into those industrialized nations that enjoy stabilized population growth along with improving economic fortunes and those Third World nations that suffer from explosive population growth and struggling economies. The solution, obviously, is to help the developing world to achieve the sort of social and economic stability found in the industrialized world; it is most certainly not for the West to enter into a three-way fertility race with the Soviet-bloc and the Third World.

UNITED NATIONS

A woman vendor at an outdoor market in Mali

A BLUEPRINT FOR SURVIVAL: RECOMMENDATIONS

The nations of the world have made real and measurable progress in the past 20 years toward controlling the growth of their populations. The efforts made over two decades by the United States and other nations to build a consensus for action in the developing world are now paying off. Population growth rates have subsided in much of Asia and Latin America. In Africa, the final holdout in population planning, five major nations have or are presently announcing comprehensive national policies to curb future growth. Ten more are in the process of drawing up such policies.

These gains, made possible by outside financial and technical assistance, will be erased without it. For anyone who doubts that fact, the experience of Pakistan is edifying. There, the dramatic advances of an early national family planning effort were all but wiped away by just a three-year suspension of government population programs in the 1970s. In 1975, just before the government suspended its efforts, fully three-quarters of Pakistani women reported knowledge of at least one method of family planning. When the next survey was taken in 1980, after the three-year lapse of efforts, that number had plunged to 26 percent.

The nations of the Third World, for all their charged commitment to curbing population growth, will fail without U.S. support. It costs money to educate far-flung, disparate rural peoples about family planning, and it costs more money to then provide them access to contraceptives and essential services. For countries already caught in the cycle of rapid population growth and sliding national economies, money is a scarce commodity.

Neither can America's industrialized allies be expected to bear the burden alone. The United States, by virtue of its history and place in the world economy, must share in the task, and it must share not only its wealth but also its knowledge and technical expertise.

For Americans prepared to take responsibility for the future world our children will inhabit, a number of steps can and should be taken immediately. Most, though not all, of them cost money, but they are all cost-effective and, in combination, they extend hope to the developing world for a better, healthier, and more stable future:

—**RESTORE U.S. POPULATION POLICY:** The United States should recommit itself to the population policy it advocated for 20 years until its reversal in Mexico City in 1984. That policy acknowledges that rapid population growth can present a significant obstacle to economic development in the Third World. It also urges developing nations to set goals for future population growth and to help families who want to limit their numbers of children to do so through voluntary family planning.

A restoration of this policy would eliminate a great deal of confusion among our allies and friends over America's 1984 about-face and would strengthen the resolve of developing nations to achieve population goals.

—**RESTORE U.S. SUPPORT FOR UNFPA**: The United States, for better or worse, has made its views clear in the international community about China's population program. Without entering the fray over whether the Chinese policy is sufficiently voluntary or whether the U.S. withdrawal was justified, it is enough to say that the United States has made its point.

WHITE HOUSE

In the White House: policy abstractions
□□□□□

The question to decide now is where to go from here. To answer that question, consider the facts. Because no U.S. funds channelled through UNFPA were used in China, the withdrawal of these funds has not stopped a single Chinese abortion. What it has done is undercut UNFPA family planning programs in more than 120 other developing nations and denied many impoverished couples the birth control they have sought. In so doing, it is almost certain that the withdrawal of U.S. funds has resulted in more unwanted pregnancies and more abortions—not in China, but in countless anonymous cities and villages around the globe. Worse yet, many of those abortions will have been dangerous self-inflicted or illegal procedures that contribute greatly to maternal mortality.

There is a strong argument to be made that the United States ought to restore funding for UNFPA programs under the original agreement by which U.S. funds went only for documented voluntary family planning services. Those who recognize the dangerous implications of a further erosion of UNFPA programs around the world will certainly see the wisdom in this. It is quite reasonable that foes of abortion should also see the wisdom in providing families with the means to prevent unwanted pregnancies and thereby avoid the necessity of confronting the agonizing dilemma of abortion.

—**RESTORE U.S. SUPPORT FOR IPPF**: For the same reasons outlined above, the United States should restore its long-standing support for the International Planned Parenthood Federation.

Just as with UNFPA, no U.S. money granted to IPPF helped to pay for abortions. Just as with UNFPA, IPPF's programs around the world are widely praised for their cost-efficiency and effectiveness. Just as with UNFPA, the United States should restore its financial support.

—RESTORE U.S. DIRECT AID FOR POPULATION PROGRAMS: Aside from U.S. assistance to international cooperative efforts like UNFPA and IPPF, the United States has also backed away from its commitment to bilateral and direct population assistance. This retreat is reflected in the consistent declines in the population budget of the U.S. Agency for International Development, which offers bilateral population assistance in 30 Third World nations. These reductions have undercut long-established U.S. and international population programs and threaten to chip away at the fragile progress made in the recent past toward controlling population growth.

The Congress should turn aside future administration efforts to reduce population assistance funds and should restore these budgets at least to their 1984 levels.

—PROMOTE COMPREHENSIVE POPULATION POLICIES ABROAD: In aiding and counseling developing countries seeking to curb population growth, the United States should continue to encourage governments to adopt a comprehensive approach. Such an approach, of course, promotes the acceptance and availability of family planning, but also includes programs to advance the status of women, encourage breastfeeding, delay age at marriage, and reduce infant mortality. Such a program, of course, also emphasizes that all efforts to limit family size must be strictly voluntary.

UNITED NATIONS

In the slums of Dhaka: wrenching poverty □□□□□

—SPUR RESEARCH & DEVELOPMENT IN NEW CONTRACEPTIVES: For some years, the federal government has been the primary financial supporter of research and development of new contraceptives. This research is important because it could well lead to safer, cheaper, more convenient, and more effective methods of birth control. Government support of this research is important because private contraceptive manufacturers would not undertake much of it without government incentives. The long-term investments required, the length of protracted government safety reviews, and the increasing difficulty of obtaining affordable liability insurance all deter companies from pressing ahead with contraceptive research and development. Therefore, it has been left to governments to take up where the corporations have left off.

Government-supported contraceptive research, in the United States and abroad, has yielded several promising products. Although each requires further testing for effectiveness and safety, each has fared quite well in preliminary tests. These products include:

Implants: Perhaps the most promising contraceptive implant is Norplant. This small capsule is implanted in a woman's upper arm and releases over time trace amounts of a hormonal contraceptive. Norplant is still undergoing U.S. trials and has yet to win approval by the U.S. Food and Drug Administration, but its use has been approved by several Western European governments and the World Health Organization, and it is already being introduced in many parts of Europe, Asia, Africa, and Latin America.

UNITED NATIONS

Family size remains large in many developing countries

There are tremendous advantages to Norplant over other contraceptives. For one thing, it is believed to be the most effective form of contraception now in use. It is also effective within 24 hours after implantation and, because it can be removed at any time by a relatively simple procedure, it is completely reversible. In addition, one implant is effective for as many as five years, which largely eliminates the difficulties in resupplying inaccessible rural areas. Thus, once a village has been serviced by a medical team and all those who desire the implant have been accommodated, there is no need to supply new contraceptives for some time, making Norplant an extremely cost-efficient method.

Research is also continuing on a second type of implant called Capronor. Capronor works in the same way as Norplant, but the smaller Capronor would last for only 18 to 24 months before dissolving into water and carbon dioxide. The fact that it naturally biodegrades eliminates the need for surgical removal.

Other Injectables: India is now testing two new injectable contraceptives for women, and doctors working on the project say the experimental drugs appear to be highly effective and so far have shown no significant ill effects in early trials. Australia is conducting similar tests on anti-pregnancy "vaccines" for women and the World Health Organization is expected to initiate its own trials this year.

Such "vaccines" would carry the same advantage of convenience promised by implants. Many couples in developing nations would be likely to accept such injections because of the known benefits and successful history of other vaccine programs administered in the Third World.

Methods for Men: Human tests on injectable contraceptives for men are set to begin this year as well, and early clinical and animal trials have been encouraging. Even so, the WHO and the National Institutes of Health, which are involved in the trials, report that they do not expect the drug to be available publicly for at least another four or five years.

Developing an effective chemical contraceptive for males has presented a special challenge because of the sheer number of sperm that must be neutralized. Wide-ranging research into new contraceptives for men over the past 20 years has met almost uniformly with frustration. Drugs that inhibit sperm production have generally been found to reduce significantly male libido and potency as well. In addition, the doses required for effectiveness are between 10 and 50 times greater than for present oral contraceptives for females, raising concerns about toxicity. Efforts to develop a reversible vasectomy have also been generally unsuccessful, although research into an implant device called "the Shug" which blocks the transport of sperm in the vas deferens has been more hopeful.

UNITED NATIONS

A rural family in Bhutan □□□□□

"Morning After" Contraceptives: Some of the most promising contraceptive research is being done on post-coital pharmaceuticals, or the so-called "morning after" pills. These pills have already been developed and have been approved for use in Great Britain and West Germany, but have not yet been approved by the U.S. FDA. In addition, France is pioneering development of an especially promising post-coital contraceptive, known as RU486.

Because "morning after" pills require higher chemical dosages for effectiveness, they are not practical as a regular contraceptive method, but are useful in events of unexpected and unprotected intercourse.

THE COST AND BENEFIT OF PROVIDING SERVICES: SOME NEW PROJECTIONS

All research into world fertility agrees on at least one conclusion: There are over 400 million people in the developing world who want to limit the size of their families, but who do not have the knowledge or the means to do so.

Perhaps the most comprehensive of this research, the World Fertility Survey and the Contraceptive Prevalence Survey, conducted in 61 nations between 1972 and 1984, found that about half of those interviewed did not want a future pregnancy. Another 25 percent said they wanted to wait for at least two years before becoming pregnant. Therefore, all tolled, 75 percent wanted to avoid pregnancy, at least for the time being.

Yet, when these same individuals were asked about their knowledge of family planning and where to obtain it, only 40 percent said they knew where to get safe and effective contraceptives. Sixty percent did not know of any family planning source.

Even the 40 percent who reported knowledge of a family planning outlet often did not have effective access. Too often, prospective family planning clients must travel long distances, not infrequently to find the outlet closed or out of supplies or too busy to see them.

Or, they may find that contraceptives are priced beyond their means. Third World couples may earn a dollar a day or less—and then only when they can find work. A month's supply of contraceptives may be too costly for them. The immediate need for food usually wins out.

The fact that more than 400 million people in the developing world want family planning services but lack the access or money to secure them is encouraging to the extent that it suggests a receptivity to reducing average family size and population growth. But it is also intimidating because it gives us some idea of the financial commitment that will be required to provide them with the services they need.

In this book, we have focused on 20 fast-growing nations that, taken together, account for 62 percent of the world's current population and 69 percent of its growth. We have calculated the probable costs in each of these nations of extending contraceptives and family planning services to all those who need and desire them.

Moreover, we have also made cost estimates for the three regions of the developing world: Africa, Asia, and Latin America. We are, therefore, able to present a global picture of prospective costs.

The time focus for this study covers the 10-year period from 1989 to 1998, a period for which programs and budgets are now being planned. During this 10-year span, the developing world will require a total of about $32 billion to provide family planning services to the couples who desire them. Because the cost models assume a reasonable progression from current program levels, the cost estimates start at $2.4 billion to provide these services globally in 1989 and rise to $4.1 billion by 1998.

The total amount of money currently being spent worldwide on family planning is difficult to assess precisely because of the multitude of funding sources, the practice among government budget writers of combining population programs with other activities, and the lack of adequate cost accounting. A budget distinction must also be made between the amount of money spent on family planning, per se, and the amount of money spent more broadly on "population programs." The cost calculations presented in this book, for the 20 developing nations highlighted and for the Third World as a whole, are based on the cost of providing *family planning* supplies and services to the people of these nations. These calculations include the actual costs of transporting these supplies, and providing access to the client populations.

UNITED NATIONS

Young children in Monrovia, Liberia
□ □ □ □ □

Currently, the international donor community spends approximately $500 million annually on population programs in the developing world, and Third World governments are spending three dollars for every one donated. The amount of money spent by the private sector—including employer contributions to family planning services, private foundations in the respective countries, and the individual couples themselves—is harder to fix, but probably totals another $200 million. That means that, altogether, roughly $2.2 billion is now being spent each year in the developing world on family planning and more broadly defined population efforts, including social-marketing campaigns, medical training of service providers, and the collection of census and certain other population data in some developing countries.

Since this book calculates that the world needs to be spending $2.4 billion annually on family planning services alone as we enter the 1990s, we estimate that roughly a billion dollars of new funds must be raised if the family planning and population goals of these nations are to be realized. Given the economic situations faced by many Third World nations, it is unrealistic to expect that they can dramatically increase their government spending over such a short period of time. Therefore, the majority of the new money needed simply must come from the international donor community. For the approximate U.S. share of that total, that would require an increase in population assistance funds to $600 million, or about twice the fiscal year 1984 appropriations for such programs.

That is a substantial amount of money. But there is a variety of sound justifications for making the investment. In addition to the very reasonable and compelling humanitarian reasons, there are national security and environmental justifications. And too often overlooked are the straightforward financial justifications. Actions to expand family planning services now may actually save the United States money in the future by making emergency relief efforts less costly.

To demonstrate that point, the Population Institute constructed a model in 1984 to determine what might have happened had Ethiopia launched a family planning program in 1970, at the same time certain other developing nations were taking such action. The model showed that a family planning program even half as effective as those in Thailand, Indonesia, or Mexico would have reduced the size of Ethiopia's 1985 population by 1.7 million—a number roughly equal to the people forced to rely on emergency food aid during that year's famine.

WORLD BANK

Suffering in Ethiopia has lessened, but the country's population problems remain

At the very time that U.S. budget planners were seeking further reductions in population assistance, they found themselves having to spend more on emergency relief efforts—programs designed to relieve the abject suffering caused in part by population pressures. In the 20 months from October 1985 through May 1987, the U.S. government spent $409 million on emergency aid to Africa.

An additional financial reason for making the investment in family planning services is the effect population growth has on economic development. It is imprudent to spend large sums of U.S. aid on economic development abroad without also working to moderate population growth. If population continues to grow faster than local economies, economic development aid is ineffective and poorly spent.

Regional Cost Estimates

Projected family planning costs by region mirror the world's population distribution. Asia contains about three-quarters of the developing world's total population, and will need about the same proportion of global family planning funds to meet regional goals.

By the same token, Africa contains about 14 percent of Third World population and Latin America about 11 percent. Cost estimates allocate about 12 percent of family planning costs to each of these regions. This division reflects the fact that somewhat more than half of Latin American couples already practice family planning, compared with only 10 percent or less in Africa.

Africa's need for family planning funds will represent an increasing share of global population funds as more and more African couples adopt family planning.

UNITED NATIONS

Women at work in Madras, India

Cost Estimates for the Twenty Nations

Cost projections for the 20 nations that have been highlighted in this study are presented in Table 1. The aggregate for the 20 countries is $29 billion—to be spent over 10 years—about half of which will be required for programs in China and India alone.

Indonesia will need about $2 billion, while Bangladesh, Brazil, and Nigeria will need more than a billion dollars each over the same period.

The Tangible Results

If the United States and the rest of the international community were to adopt the plan of action outlined in this book, the positive results would be nothing less than astounding.

The bottom line is that if the world is willing to make the modest investments necessary, the earth less than 50 years from now will be 3.2 billion people smaller than if we do not step up our efforts.

Table II outlines the slow-down of world and regional population growth if the recommendations in this book are adopted and achieved. This calculation shows world population eventually stabilizing around the middle of the next century. The outlook presented in these figures is far brighter than the outlook if the recommendations are not adopted.

The difference in sheer numbers will be substantial, and yet the goals we have assumed are not exceedingly ambitious. They call for the roughly 100 developing nations with average family sizes now higher than four children to bring that average down to just four children.

If the level of family planning activity envisioned in these models is realized, none of these 100 countries will have a Total Fertility Rate higher than 4 by the year 2000. Furthermore, aggregate regional fertility rates for Asia and Latin America will resemble those found in developed nations. (The Total Fertility Rate for more developed countries is now 1.9 children per woman.)

If family planning efforts continue to expand at current rates into the next century, African couples could also achieve a Total Fertility Rate of 1.9 as early as 2010.

The alternative projection assumes that fertility rates around the world will continue to decline gradually and that the world will continue its modest efforts to extend family planning services. Our projection assumes a more committed effort and shows the results.

If the developing nations with family averages of more than four children successfully reduce that average to four children per family by the year 2000, as provided in this book's recommendations, there would then be approximately 200 million fewer people in the world. By 2010, there would be almost 750 million fewer people, and by 2030, the world would be fully 3.2 billion people smaller than if these nations maintained current family sizes averaging larger than four children.

UNITED NATIONS

In Ethiopia, fresh water must be trucked in
□ □ □ □ □

One might be tempted to assume that the difference between the two projections is really not great; after all, with a world population upwards of 7 billion people, what difference does another billion, or two or three, really make?

It could make a world of difference. Even one extra billion people could push regional populations over the threshold of local carrying capacities and spark severe environmental or economic deterioration. The world already will be hard pressed to accommodate 7 billion people without irreparable damage to its environment and economy; pushing that number to 9 billion, 10 billion, or beyond could be disastrous.

The projections contained here for population growth based on extension of family planning services over the next several decades to all those who want them are truly encouraging. They depend, of course, upon the willingness of the United States and other donor nations to increase their financial commitments as outlined earlier. These data suggest that with sufficient international support world population growth can be brought into a more liveable pattern within a relatively short period of time.

If the United States and other donor nations were to adopt the policy and spending recommendations contained in this book, it is fair to assume that a portion of the new money would be spent in bilateral, or government-to-government, aid. Much of the new money, however, would need to be spent through international intermediary organizations. This is because a number of Third World nations are sensitive to the political implications of accepting direct assistance from a foreign government such as the United States. It is also because channeling international contributions through multi-lateral service providers allows for a centralization of priorities and minimizes duplication of effort. That fact, combined with their special ability to work cooperatively with indigenous groups, helps to speed the delivery of services and ensure the efficiency of program implementation.

INTERNATIONAL SERVICE PROVIDERS

It may be useful, therefore, to take a somewhat closer look at the largest and most influential organizations involved in the delivery of population assistance and family planning services in Third World countries.

The Major Agencies

United Nations Fund for Population Activities (UNFPA):

The UNFPA is the largest and most comprehensive provider of international population assistance. Since its inception in 1969, UNFPA has worked in 141 developing countries and these projects have been funded by voluntary contributions from more than 100 countries worldwide. While the U.N. agency receives most of its funds from industrialized donor nations, many developing countries also make contributions, even if the small amounts can only serve as an expression of their concern and commitment.

UNFPA's annual budget of approximately $150 million is used to help Third World governments to develop effective national population policies and goals. UNFPA creates awareness of the problems caused by rapid or uneven population growth as well as the possible solutions to those problems. It supports a wide range of population-related projects, including the delivery of family planning services, assistance for national censuses and basic data collection, and population information and education. Nearly three-quarters of UNFPA's budget goes toward country projects and two-thirds of the agency's international assistance is spent in the world's 65 poorest nations.

The UNFPA lost its largest contributor and traditionally its strongest supporter in 1986, when the United States cut off its aid to the agency. Following the U.S. withdrawal, several other donor nations, including Canada, Japan, and Finland, increased their contributions by a cumulative total of $10 million, but the shortfall remains significant because the United States had originally pledged $46 million.

The U.S. action has limited UNFPA's efforts just as the agency announced in 1987 its new funding priorities. As UNFPA looks ahead to the 1990s, its priority programs will be oriented to (1) sub-Saharan Africa, (2) improving the status of women worldwide, and (3) training that leads to the self-sufficiency of programs in the developing world.

A closer look at the important and now uncertain relationship between the United States and UNFPA is provided in the separate article, "The Global Blow," accompanying this section.

FAO

Pregnant woman in Dahomey

UNFPA is based at 220 East 42nd Street, New York, New York 10017; telephone (212) 850-5631.

International Planned Parenthood Federation (IPPF):

IPPF is the global umbrella organization for 104 private affiliates worldwide, including the U.S.-based Planned Parenthood Federation of America. IPPF works actively in most developing nations to extend family planning services and contraceptive availability to the rural and urban poor.

The London-based organization is funded through private contributions through its affiliate members and traditionally receives substantial support from the governments of more than 20 nations, including the United Kingdom, Sweden, Denmark, Australia, and Japan. Although the U.S. government, which had been IPPF's largest contributor, has suspended its support of IPPF's central organization in London since 1985, the United States still contributes to IPPF's Western Hemisphere division based in New York City.

IPPF is headquartered at Regent's College, Inner Circle, Regent's Park, London NW1 4NS, England; telephone (441) 486-0741. IPPF's Western Hemisphere division is located at 902 Broadway, New York, New York 10010; telephone (212) 995-8800.

Family Planning International Assistance (FPIA):

FPIA was organized in 1971 as the international assistance arm of the Planned Parenthood Federation of America. Funded almost

(continued on page 98)

The Global Blow: Defunding of UNFPA

More than 95 percent of the people in the developing world, where virtually all of the earth's population growth now occurs, live in countries that have adopted policies to limit their human numbers.

These policies resulted from the determination of individual Third World leaders to avert the consequences that rapid demographic expansion portends for the health, environment and the quality of life of their people.

Most of these poor nations, where life is too frequently a day-to-day struggle for survival, are unable to meet the substantial and growing demand for family planning services without generous support from industrialized countries.

The United Nations Fund for Population Activities is the most important agency providing family planning assistance to the developing world. A multilateral organization established in 1969—largely through the encouragement of the United States—the UNFPA has worked to help some 140 governments achieve their fertility goals.

From the inception of the UNFPA until 1985, the United States appropriated approximately $400 million, or 26 percent of the U.N. agency's total budget, to that organization. In 1981, the U.S. Congress earmarked 16 percent of all U.S. population assistance for the UNFPA.

Four years later, the U.S. Agency for International Development, through which U.S. contributions to the UNFPA are channeled, announced that for the first time it would not provide any assistance to the Fund.

The decision marked the culmination of the Administration's efforts to change the United States' long-standing policy of support for international population assistance—one that had the endorsement of five U.S. Presidents and more than 20 years of bipartisan backing in Congress.

Shortly after Ronald Reagan moved into the White House, his Administration—spurred by groups opposed to both modern contraception and abortion—sought to eliminate the entire international population budget. After the backroom plan was discovered and promptly thwarted, anti-family planning forces developed a new strategy: to prevent U.S. funding of the most effective providers of contraceptive services to Third World countries.

The first target was the Boston-based Pathfinder Fund, established to assist international population programs by the late family planning pioneer Dr. Clarence Gamble. Threatened with losing all U.S. government financial support, Pathfinder agreed that it would remove all abortion activities from its overseas programs (even though these activities were funded entirely by private sources).

The first actual victim was the International Planned Parenthood Federation. The Administration decided that U.S. support would be withdrawn from IPPF because less than one half of one per cent of the private voluntary organization's funds, generated from non-government sources, were used for abortions.

The Administration then turned its attention to the UNFPA.

In 1984, a total of $19 million, one half of the U.S. amount earmarked for the UNFPA that year, was withheld by the Administration on grounds that it needed "concrete assurances" that the Fund does not support abortion or coercive family planning programs.

The U.S. contribution, ordinarily presented to the U.N. organization during the early months of the year, was withheld until August of 1984 when AID Administrator M. Peter McPherson received a letter from the late UNFPA Executive Director Rafael M. Salas which repeated the same "concrete assurances" Salas had enunciated in a letter he had sent to McPherson four months earlier.

Anti-family planning groups continued to focus on the UNFPA because of its assistance to the Chinese family planning program, which allegedly encouraged forced abortions and sterilizations. (The Chinese government has adamantly claimed that its program is wholly voluntary.) The UNFPA repeatedly insisted that it does not support coercive abortion activities in China or anywhere else in the world. But to prevent a recurrence of charges that it uses U.S. dollars to support the Chinese program, the UNFPA agreed to separate all future U.S. contributions into a special account to ensure that none were being used in China.

In March of 1985, the U.S. Agency for International Development completed a review of UNFPA and its policies, and concluded:

> "There is no evidence that UNFPA is intentionally or actually promoting abortions in any country, either in its 1984 program or in its proposed 1985 commitments . . . UNFPA does not support abortion or coercion through the program that our 1985 contribution would help fund. Its program is substantially in compliance with U.S. law and policy on population assistance."

On the final day of the same month, AID Administrator McPherson announced that the Administration would provide only $36 million of the $46 million earmarked for the UNFPA in the fiscal 1985 foreign aid appropriations bill. The $10 million withheld was equal to the Fund's annual contribution to the program in China.

McPherson's rationale for his decision was an amendment to the 1985 supplemental appropriations bill. Sponsored by Rep. Jack F. Kemp (R–N.Y.), the measure restricted U.S. funds from going to any organization that "supports or participates in the management of a program of coercive abortion or involuntary sterilization."

In September of 1986, the Agency for International Development announced its decision to deny the UNFPA the $25 million for fiscal year 1986 authorized by Congress. The Kemp amendment was once again cited as the justification for the action.

Congress included $32 million for the UNFPA in its fiscal 1987 continuing resolution for federal spending. In its request for funding for the UNFPA, the Administration made the following comment:

> "AID's contribution to UNFPA is important because of that organization's ability to work in countries which prefer multilateral donor assistance and because of the complementary resources it provides to countries where AID has bilateral programs."

Yet, at the same time that justification for future funding was being advanced, maneuvers were underway to maintain the U.S. ban on support to UNFPA. The contradictory messages projected by the Administration, as well as the disruption the United States has caused to a popular, multi-lateral effort has confused important U.S. allies. The United States for many years stood shoulder-to-shoulder with the nations of Western Europe and the Third World and provided respected leadership in an international cause. Suddenly, the United States has changed course and left its friends to carry the burden alone.

The future relationship between the United States and UNFPA will help determine the world's success in stabilizing rapid population growth. At the moment, that future remains anything but clear.

entirely by U.S. government grants, FPIA currently operates in 36 developing countries, and over its history has assisted more than 50 nations.

FPIA's projects are designed to establish smaller-scale, low-technology family planning delivery systems in developing countries, with an emphasis on self-sufficiency so that the programs can continue to operate after FPIA terminates funding and withdraws. The programs take special advantage of existing indigenous organizations as delivery vehicles, including church, women's, and health associations.

In addition to its delivery projects, FPIA provides contraceptive supplies to more than 100 developing countries.

FPIA is based at 810 Seventh Avenue, New York, New York 10019; telephone (212) 541-7800.

FAO

Fuelwood is getting scarcer. Loss of trees creates new deserts

The Pathfinder Fund:

The Pathfinder Fund is a private, non-profit organization founded in 1957 by the late family planning pioneer Dr. Clarence Gamble. The Boston-based Fund promotes family planning programs throughout the developing world and has helped to establish national family planning associations in several Asian, Latin American, and African nations. It also counsels developing world governments and private institutions in the development of policies conducive to the expanded availability and acceptance of contraceptives.

In addition to its efforts to build family planning delivery systems in the Third World, the Pathfinder Fund assists in the training of medical professionals from developing nations, and promotes population information and education projects abroad.

The Pathfinder Fund was once funded entirely from private sources, but now receives nearly 90 percent of its budget from the U.S. government. After the threatened withdrawal of U.S. government funds in 1984, the Fund was forced to change its policy of using privately raised funds to offer abortion as a part of its population-related programs abroad.

The Pathfinder Fund is located at 9 Galen Street, Suite 217, Watertown, Massachusetts 02172; telephone (617) 924-7200.

Association for Voluntary Surgical Contraception (AVSC):

Founded in 1943 and funded in large part by U.S. government

contracts, AVSC works in the United States and more than 60 developing countries to extend the availability of sterilization as an option for those couples who have reached their desired family-size.

A non-profit membership organization, AVSC assists in the delivery of voluntary sterilization services, the training of Third World medical personnel in modern surgical contraception, the maintenance of medical equipment, and quality assurance efforts to guarantee the safety and efficiency of participating clinics.

AVSC has convened several international conferences on voluntary surgical contraception and helped in the establishment of more than 30 national associations for voluntary surgical contraception in the developing world. AVSC also helps to support the World Federation of Health Agencies for the Advancement of Voluntary Surgical Contraception, an international organization founded in 1975 by a group of national family planning associations.

AVSC is located at 122 East 42nd Street, New York, New York 10168; telephone (212) 351-2500.

Family Health International (FHI):

Family Health International is a non-profit research and training institution based in North Carolina's academic and research triangle. In its early years, FHI focused its research efforts entirely on new contraceptive technologies. FHI still conducts extensive research into safer and more effective contraceptives, but now has broadened its scope to include studies of community-based health care delivery, infant and maternal mortality, and hospital maternity services.

FAO

Africa must import much of its food
□ □ □ □ □

FHI also offers training to physicians and medical personnel from developing countries in new contraceptive technologies and administration of health care services. FHI draws on an international network of collaborating investigators for its projects in the Third World and receives support and contracts from the U.S. Agency for International Development.

FHI's headquarters are located at Research Triangle Park, North Carolina 27709; telephone (919) 544-7040.

Development Associates, Inc.:

Development Associates is a private consulting firm based in the Washington, D.C., area. Development Associates advises businesses, schools, governments, and non-profit organizations on projects ranging from health care and rural development to education and drug use. Under contracts with the U.S. Agency for International Development, the firm provides training and technical expertise to medical personnel and family planning workers in the developing world, particularly in Latin America and the Caribbean.

Many of the firm's population-related projects are focused on training workers in Latin American rural areas to be able to counsel and provide basic family planning services to their local communities.

Development Associates, Inc., is based at 2924 Columbia Pike, Arlington, Virginia 22204; telephone (703) 979-0100.

UNITED NATIONS

Bolivian mother and child

The Futures Group:

The Futures Group is a Connecticut-based, for-profit corporation with offices in Washington specializing in commercial marketing and long-range futures modeling. Having won several major U.S. government contracts, the Futures Group has applied its wider modeling and marketing experience to the population field, where it has worked to develop contraceptive social marketing programs and government population policies in Third World nations.

The Futures Group's social marketing programs promote through commercial channels the wider and more effective use of contraceptives in the Third World and are designed to suit the specific cultural conditions of the countries in which they operate.

The Futures Group's Washington office is located at 1101 14th Street, N.W., 3rd Floor, Washington, D.C. 20005; telephone (202) 347-8165.

The Population Council:

Founded in 1952, the Population Council is a private and highly respected non-profit research organization based in New York City. The Council's Center for Biomedical Research works to develop safer and more effective methods of contraception, and led research efforts in the newly developed Norplant contraceptive for women. The Council's Center for Policy Studies conducts social science research aimed at developing more effective government policies on population. Finally, the Council's International Programs division provides technical assistance overseas to promote wider understanding of population issues.

The Population Council is based at One Dag Hammarskjold Plaza, New York, New York 10017; telephone (212) 644-1760.

Population Information Program:

The Population Information Program of The Johns Hopkins University School of Hygiene and Public Health advances public understanding of population issues under U.S. government grants. The Program publishes a journal, *Population Reports*, five times yearly, covering developments in the population field and contraceptive research.

The Population Communication Services division helps to promote understanding and awareness of family planning options and benefits in developing nations. It also designs education and marketing programs to match specific Third World countries.

The Hopkins Population Communication Services program helped direct the highly successful marketing in Mexico of a song in which the popular Mexican vocal duo of "Johnny and Tatiana" urged teenagers to delay sexual activity. Similar projects are underway in Asia and Africa. Currently, the Hopkins center is emphasizing new efforts in Africa.

The Population Information Program is located at the Center for Communication Programs, The Johns Hopkins University, 527 St. Paul Place, Baltimore, Maryland 21202; telephone (301) 659-6300.

FAO

Mothers tend market in southern Mexico
□ □ □ □ □

The Centre for Development and Population Activities (CEDPA):

Founded in 1975, CEDPA is a private, non-profit organization dedicated to improving the managerial and technical capabilities of women in the Third World. The Washington, D.C.-based organization holds intensive five-week training workshops in the United States for Third World women who are mid- to senior-level managers of family planning, health care, or development programs in their home countries. The workshops are conducted in the native languages of the participants and are designed to help propel women to higher levels of responsibility in Third World population and development efforts.

CEDPA now has a network of more than 2,000 "alumni" throughout the developing world. CEDPA utilizes its alumni network to implement other family planning and community health care projects in the developing world.

CEDPA's offices are at 1717 Massachusetts Avenue, N.W., Suite 202, Washington, D.C. 20036; telephone (202) 667-1142.

International Council on the Management of Population Programmes (ICOMP):

ICOMP is an organization founded by the directors of Third World population and family planning programs. ICOMP concentrates its efforts on improving the management of health care and family planning programs in the developing world by offering technical expertise and training, as well as encouraging the exchange of ideas and information among the various national programs.

ICOMP is funded by a number of governments—mainly from the industrialized donor community—international organizations, and private foundations. It has conducted fact-finding missions to developing countries, especially in Africa, to identify areas needing special assistance, and has organized a series of international workshops bringing together the managers of regional and national population programs.

The Council is headquartered at 141 Jalan Dahlia, Taman Uda Jaya, 68000 Ampang, Kuala Lumpur, Malaysia; telephone (603) 457-3234.

U.S. AID

Families look for help

Japanese Organization for International Cooperation in Family Planning (JOICFP):

JOICFP was founded in 1968 by Japanese family planning experts to promote Japanese assistance in international population and maternal and child health projects.

JOICFP is a non-governmental organization, but works closely with the Japanese government, UNFPA, and other international population organizations. JOICFP works domestically to encourage greater awareness and concern within Japan about rapid world population growth and is active in projects to extend family planning, nutrition, and public health services in Asia, Africa, and Latin America. It also organizes international workshops and publishes informational materials and several respected journals covering global population issues.

JOICFP is located at Hoken Kaikan Bekkan, Sixth Floor, 1-1 Sadohara-cho, Tokyo 162, Japan.

United Nations Children's Fund (UNICEF):

In addition to UNICEF's extensive work to advance the general health and welfare of children, the U.N. agency also promotes family planning in the developing world. This effort arises from UNICEF's recognition that rapid population growth and improper child-spacing contribute significantly to infant and child mortality.

The UNICEF Executive Board in 1987 set the goal of cutting infant mortality rates in half by the year 2000, and named proper child-spacing made possible through family planning as a key means of achieving that goal.

UNICEF is headquartered at 866 United Nations Plaza, New York, New York 10017; telephone (212) 415-8000.

World Health Organization (WHO):

The World Health Organization is the division of the United Nations charged with coordinating U.N. efforts to improve the health of all people internationally. The WHO considers family planning to be an essential part of the comprehensive health services it seeks to promote globally.

WHO recognizes the serious consequences of rapid population growth for public health and works to extend the availability of contraceptives and family planning services through its wide-ranging delivery of health care in the developing world. The Geneva-based organization also conducts independent research into new contraceptive technologies.

FAO

In Senegal, day care can mean a box □□□□□

WHO's headquarters are at 1211 Geneva 27, Switzerland; telephone (91) 2111. WHO's main U.S. office is located at 525 23rd Street, N.W., Washington, D.C. 20037; telephone (202) 861-3248.

Management Counseling Programs:

The U.S. government also funds projects to improve the management systems of Third World population programs. In this regard, the government utilizes three principal contractors: John Snow, Inc., John Short and Associates, and the Boston-based Management Sciences for Health.

These management consultants work with the administrators of both private and government-run family planning programs in developing countries to identify and correct program weaknesses and provide technical and management training to personnel. They also promote greater participation among Third World businesses and private health care providers in the local delivery of family planning services.

John Snow, Inc., is headquartered at 210 Lincoln Street, Boston, Massachusetts 02111; telephone (617) 482-9485. John Short and Associates, Inc., is based at 10320 Little Patuxent Parkway, The Equitable Bank Center, Suite 1002, Columbia, Maryland 21044; telephone (301) 964-2811. Management Sciences for Health is headquartered at 165 Allandale Road, Boston, Massachusetts 02130; telephone (617) 524-7799.

UNITED NATIONS

Woman and child in Sudan

A CALL TO ACTION: CONCLUSIONS

The United States cannot solve the problem of rapid world population growth by simply "throwing money at it." The problem is far too difficult and complex for that.

Moreover, the United States can certainly not solve the problem by any unilateral effort. Ultimately, it is up to the developing world to win the fight for stable population growth. To that end, 45 heads of state from the developing world have demonstrated their willingness and commitment to a solution by signing the Statement on Population Stabilization. This historic agreement, which was presented to the 100th Congress of the United States on April 24, 1987, is printed in full as Appendix A.

In it, the leaders of some of the largest and most populous Third World nations agreed:

"Degradation of the world's environment, income inequality, and the potential for conflict exist today because of over-consumption and over-population. If this unprecedented population growth continues, future generations of children will not have adequate food, housing, medical care, education, earth resources, and employment opportunities. We believe the time has come now to recognize the world-wide necessity to stop population growth within the near future and for each country to adopt the necessary policies and programs to do so."

This agreement is vitally important because it represents one of the three basic ingredients required for progress toward an end to the world's population crisis: political leadership. Given sufficient political leadership, the other two ingredients—the availability of contraceptives and the motivation to use them—will follow. But the above declaration represents only one half of the political leadership necessary: that from the developing world. The other half—sustained and far-sighted political leadership in the industrialized world and the international donor community—must be proven anew.

While it is not the sole responsibility of the United States to solve the problem, it is most certainly America's responsibility to help. The United States can make a pivotal contribution toward an eventual solution by rejoining the international partnership it once led.

It is true that responsible action, as outlined in these recommendations, will require more money than has been committed in recent years by the United States. And, in an era of fiscal restraint and painful budget cutbacks, it is fair to seek a rigorous justification for such spending. The Congress must ask hard questions about U.S. population policy and spending, because effective progress depends not only on the size of budgets, but also on how wisely those budgets are spent.

The status of women, infant mortality, age at marriage, breastfeeding and other factors all play important roles in influencing fertility and population growth. But the most effective way to reduce population growth is to do it directly: to extend to couples the information and access to family planning so that they may decide for themselves the number of their children.

Unlike building a new interstate highway or a new weapons system, spending on population programs cannot be successfully deferred. We have very real opportunities before us to wrestle population growth into a more stable pattern. The solution, built upon 20 years of international cooperation and investment, is within reach. But these opportunities exist now, in our world of 5 billion people and still-plentiful natural resources. If we choose not to grasp these opportunities, they will slip away. If we decide to wait until the world swells to 6 billion or 8 billion people (we will reach the former in less than 9 years) and until overpopulation and poverty have ravaged the natural and economic resources of the Third World, it will be too late.

WORLD BANK

Malawi: Women tend to children and field. Women do 2/3 of the world's work and earn 1/10 of its income
□ □ □ □ □

If Americans now feel anguish over witnessing the recent human suffering and needless deaths in Ethiopia, just imagine a world in which virtually the entire Third World will be wracked by vast poverty and human misery.

If Americans now think they have a problem with illegal immigration, imagine a world in which spreading despair will create tremendous new pressures on U.S. borders, especially from Latin America and the Caribbean.

And if Americans are now troubled by the specter of instability, revolution, and authoritarianism in the Third World, they have only to imagine the consequences of inaction, because the fragile seed of democracy cannot survive long in societies with escalating misery, crippled economies, and dying environments.

In shaping the federal budget, the U.S. Congress must ask not only how much it will cost to fund population programs, but also what will be the costs of *not* funding them. The investment required now is modest by any standard. And the returns will be great because in helping developing nations to control their population growth, the United States will also build stronger economies and friendships in the strategically important Third World.

If we do not act, however, or if our actions are inadequate, no amount of U.S. dollars later will be able to break the powerful cycle of overpopulation, economic and environmental deterioration, and human despair.

The United States has built an enviable record of far-sighted and compassionate leadership in the struggle for international development. Our allies and friends in the Third World now look to us to see what we will do. The stakes are no less than the survival of our planet. But our opportunities to shape a better future are just as great.

Whether we seize them, and what kind of world is in store for our children and grandchildren, depends upon how we respond now. The future is up to us.

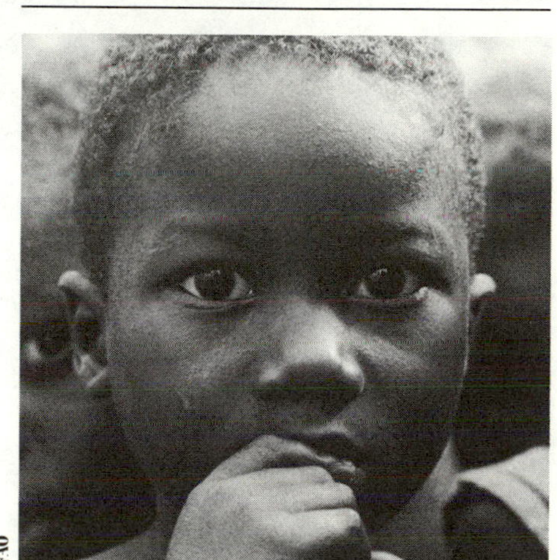

FAO

Looking to the future
□ □ □ □ □

Founded in 1969, The Population Institute is the largest private, non-profit organization working for a more equitable balance between the earth's population, its environment, and its resources.

The Institute does not receive, nor does it seek, any financial support from the United States government. The Institute is supported by grants from more than 50 private foundations and more than 30,000 individual donors. As a tax-exempt 501(c)(3), non-profit organization, all contributions are tax deductible.

With more than 40,000 participating members beyond its 30,000 individual donors, The Population Institute is headquartered on Capitol Hill in Washington, D.C., and has offices in Brussels, Belgium; Colombo, Sri Lanka; and Bogota, Colombia.

All proceeds from the sale of this book will go to the Population Institute to support its international efforts to promote awareness of rapid population growth and humane and responsible population policies around the globe.

ABOUT THE POPULATION INSTITUTE

STATEMENT ON POPULATION STABILIZATION BY WORLD LEADERS

Mankind has many challenges: to obtain a lasting peace between nations; to preserve the quality of the environment; to conserve resources at a sustainable level; to advance the economic and social progress of the less developed nations, and to stabilize population growth.

At present there are 76 million more births than deaths on our planet each year. If present rates continue, by the year 2000, there will be 100 million more births than deaths. A billion people have been added in the last 13 years and the next billion will be added in 12 years.

Degradation of the world environment, income inequality, and the potential for conflict exist today because of over-consumption and over-population. If this unprecedented population growth continues, future generations of children will not have adequate food, housing, medical care, education, earth resources, and employment opportunities.

This declaration was presented to the 100th U.S. Congress with the assistance and support of the Global Committee of Parliamentarians on Population and Development and The Population Institute.

We believe that the time has come now to recognize the world-wide necessity to stop population growth within the near future and for each country to adopt the necessary policies and programs to do so, consistent with its own culture and aspirations.

To enhance the integrity of the individual and the quality of life for all, we believe that all nations should participate in setting goals and programs for population stabilization. Measures for this purpose should be voluntary and should maintain individual human rights and beliefs.

We urge national leaders to take an active personal role in promoting effective policies and programs. Attention should be given to setting realistic goals and timetables; encouraging active participation of communities in designing and implementing their own programs; and developing appropriate economic and social policies.

We call upon donor nations and institutions to be more generous in their support of population programs in those developing nations requesting such assistance.

Recognizing that early population stabilization is in the interest of all nations, we earnestly hope that leaders around the world will share our views and join with us in this great undertaking for the well-being and happiness of people everywhere.

Austria	Fiji	Liberia	St. Kitts-Nevis
Bangladesh	Grenada	Malta	St. Lucia—West Indies
Barbados	Guinea-Bissau	Mauritius	St. Vincent and the Grenadines
Bhutan	Haiti	Morocco	Sudan
Botswana	Iceland	Nepal	Thailand
Cape Verde	India	Nigeria	Tonga
China	Indonesia	Panama	Tunisia
Cyprus	Jamaica	Philippines	Vanuatu
Dominica	Japan	Rwanda	Zimbabwe
Dominican Republic	Jordan	Senegal	
Egypt	Kenya	Seychelles	
	Korea	Sri Lanka	

□ □ □ □ □

TABLE I: Family Planning Costs in 20 Countries: 1989 to 1998 ($ million)

Country	Total	1989	1990	1991	1992	1993	1994	1995	1996	1997	1998	1989–93	1994–98
Total	28,983	2,150	2,311	2,493	2,654	2,815	2,977	3,136	3,310	3,487	3,650	12,423	16,560
Bangladesh	1,431	92	102	116	127	138	150	160	170	182	193	575	855
Brazil	1,376	124	126	126	130	134	138	143	147	151	155	641	735
Burma	337	19	21	25	28	32	35	39	43	46	49	125	212
China	8,676	706	736	767	803	840	878	926	972	1,007	1,041	3,852	4,824
Egypt	569	37	40	45	50	55	59	64	70	73	77	226	342
Ethiopia	559	38	42	46	49	53	57	61	66	72	77	228	332
India	6,374	459	511	570	600	632	663	691	718	749	781	2,772	3,603
Indonesia	2,012	162	174	182	191	199	208	205	214	234	243	908	1,105
Iran	503	32	36	40	44	48	52	56	61	65	69	200	303
Kenya	317	18	22	25	28	31	33	36	39	42	42	124	193
Korea, South	575	49	51	52	54	56	58	61	63	65	66	263	312
Mexico	943	77	81	86	90	94	98	99	101	106	111	428	515
Nigeria	1,223	59	68	83	99	115	130	145	160	174	189	425	798
Pakistan	920	58	64	70	77	84	91	100	113	125	138	353	567
Philippines	611	44	48	52	56	60	64	67	70	74	78	259	352
Tanzania	316	15	19	22	25	29	34	38	42	45	48	110	206
Thailand	565	49	50	51	53	55	57	59	62	64	66	258	307
Turkey	653	46	50	54	58	63	67	71	76	81	87	271	382
Vietnam	639	44	48	52	57	62	66	70	75	80	85	262	376
Zaire	386	22	25	29	32	36	40	44	48	52	56	144	241

Source: The Population Institute, 1987.

□ □ □ □ □

TABLE II: Population Projections Based on Achievement of Fertility Goals (in 1000s)

Year	Africa	Asia	Latin America	MDCs	LDCs	World
1980	484,188	2,573,131	356,590	1,139,476	3,413,909	4,553,385
1985	565,099	2,820,247	400,510	1,162,818	3,785,856	4,948,674
1990	654,974	3,065,812	445,154	1,182,665	4,165,940	5,348,605
1995	748,841	3,294,922	485,970	1,197,952	4,529,733	5,727,685
2000	839,680	3,486,319	520,062	1,209,477	4,846,061	6,055,538
2005	920,411	3,648,538	550,145	1,212,442	5,119,094	6,331,536
2010	986,257	3,803,386	580,230	1,207,356	5,369,873	6,577,229
2015	1,042,327	3,944,628	608,046	1,198,173	5,595,001	6,793,174
2020	1,095,729	4,060,582	630,807	1,184,280	5,787,118	6,971,398
2025	1,148,196	4,143,191	647,191	1,165,657	5,938,578	7,104,235
2030	1,194,394	4,192,725	657,822	1,140,216	6,044,941	7,185,157

Key: "MDCs" refers to "More Developed Countries," or the nations of the industrialized world. "LDCs" refers to "Less Developed Countries," or the nations of the developing world.

Source: The Population Institute, 1987.

□ □ □ □ □

TABLE III: Cost of Expanding Family Planning in Developing Nations: 1989 to 1998 ($ million)

Country	Total	1989	1990	1991	1992	1993	1994	1995	1996	1997	1998	1989–93	1994–98
Total LDCs	**32,827**	**2,427**	**2,617**	**2,825**	**3,004**	**3,195**	**3,370**	**3,557**	**3,739**	**3,949**	**4,145**	**14,067**	**18,760**
In Study	28,983	2,150	2,311	2,493	2,654	2,815	2,977	3,136	3,310	3,487	3,650	12,423	16,560
Other	3,844	278	305	332	350	379	394	421	429	462	495	1,643	2,201
Africa LDCs	**3,956**	**217**	**249**	**292**	**333**	**376**	**416**	**458**	**495**	**540**	**579**	**1,467**	**2,489**
In Study	3,369	189	215	250	284	319	353	388	424	459	489	1,257	2,112
Other	587	28	35	42	49	57	63	71	70	81	91	210	376
Asia LDCs	**25,057**	**1,887**	**2,032**	**2,186**	**2,310**	**2,443**	**2,565**	**2,697**	**2,833**	**2,982**	**3,121**	**10,858**	**14,198**
In Study	23,296	1,760	1,890	2,031	2,150	2,268	2,388	2,506	2,637	2,772	2,895	10,098	13,197
Other	1,761	128	142	155	160	175	177	191	195	211	226	760	1,001
Latin America LDCs	**3,815**	**323**	**335**	**347**	**361**	**376**	**389**	**401**	**412**	**427**	**444**	**1,742**	**2,073**
In Study	2,319	201	207	212	220	228	236	242	249	257	266	1,069	1,250
Other	1,496	122	128	135	140	148	153	159	163	170	178	673	823

Key: "LDCs" refers to Less Developed Countries.
Source: The Population Institute, 1987.

□ □ □ □ □

TABLE IV: Contraceptive Supplies Needed to Expand Family Planning: 1989 to 1998

Year	All LDCs	Africa	Asia	Latin America	Africa	Asia	Latin America
Monthly Cycles of Oral Contraceptives (1,000 Cycles)							
Total	7,926,584	1,214,362	5,382,457	1,329,765	15.3%	67.9%	16.8%
1989	671,286	76,559	469,076	125,651	11.4%	69.9%	18.7%
1990	715,499	84,127	503,616	127,757	11.8%	70.4%	17.9%
1991	737,770	94,540	513,088	130,141	12.8%	69.5%	17.6%
1992	758,998	105,088	521,606	132,305	13.8%	68.7%	17.4%
1993	779,312	115,787	529,307	134,219	14.9%	67.9%	17.2%
1994	798,715	126,553	536,305	135,856	15.8%	67.1%	17.0%
1995	817,214	137,343	542,683	137,188	16.8%	66.4%	16.8%
1996	855,013	147,995	570,372	136,646	17.3%	66.7%	16.0%
1997	883,167	158,247	589,197	135,695	17.9%	66.7%	15.4%
1998	909,611	168,097	607,207	134,307	18.5%	66.8%	14.8%
1989-93	3,662,865	476,101	2,536,692	650,072	13.0%	69.3%	17.7%
1994-98	4,263,720	738,262	2,845,765	679,693	17.3%	66.7%	15.9%
Pre-sterilized IUD Kits (1,000 Kits)							
Total	112,635	10,062	98,664	3,909	8.9%	87.6%	3.5%
1989	11,561	791	10,394	376	6.8%	89.9%	3.2%
1990	11,828	858	10,581	389	7.3%	89.5%	3.3%
1991	12,169	901	10,860	408	7.4%	89.2%	3.4%
1992	12,167	952	10,805	410	7.8%	88.8%	3.4%
1993	12,165	1,000	10,754	411	8.2%	88.4%	3.4%
1994	12,172	1,054	10,708	410	8.7%	88.0%	3.4%

□ □ □ □ □

TABLE IV: (Continued)

Year	All LDCs	Africa	Asia	Latin America	Africa	Asia	Latin America
Pre-sterilized IUD Kits (1,000 Kits) (continued)							
1995	11,454	1,093	9,963	398	9.5%	87.0%	3.5%
1996	10,299	1,122	8,796	380	10.9%	85.4%	3.7%
1997	9,617	1,141	8,107	370	11.9%	84.3%	3.8%
1998	9,204	1,150	7,697	357	12.5%	83.6%	3.9%
1989-93	59,889	4,503	53,394	1,993	7.5%	89.2%	3.3%
1994-98	52,746	5,560	45,271	1,916	10.5%	85.8%	3.6%
Condoms (1,000 pieces)							
Total	51,419,609	9,752,283	36,201,840	5,465,486	19.0%	70.4%	10.6%
1989	2,959,082	427,971	2,217,258	313,853	14.5%	74.9%	10.6%
1990	3,407,193	529,152	2,516,293	361,749	15.5%	73.9%	10.6%
1991	3,858,311	634,747	2,815,092	408,472	16.5%	73.0%	10.6%
1992	4,334,549	750,015	3,126,323	458,211	17.3%	72.1%	10.6%
1993	4,837,218	876,313	3,449,892	511,014	18.1%	71.3%	10.6%
1994	5,366,279	1,013,491	3,785,862	566,927	18.9%	70.5%	10.6%
1995	5,922,676	1,162,209	4,134,472	625,995	19.6%	69.8%	10.6%
1996	6,355,460	1,302,106	4,372,296	681,058	20.5%	68.8%	10.7%
1997	6,903,523	1,449,982	4,714,702	738,839	21.0%	68.3%	10.7%
1998	7,475,318	1,606,299	5,069,651	799,368	21.5%	67.8%	10.7%
1989-93	19,396,354	3,218,197	14,124,857	2,053,299	16.6%	72.8%	10.6%
1994-98	32,023,255	6,534,086	22,076,983	3,412,186	20.4%	68.9%	10.7%

Source: The Population Institute, 1987.

INDEX